BORDEN®
135TH ANNIVERSARY
COOKBOOK

Appetizers & Beverages

REALEMONADE

Makes about 1 quart

1/2 cup sugar
1/2 cup ReaLemon® Lemon Juice
   from Concentrate
3 1/4 cups cold water
   Ice

In pitcher, dissolve sugar in ReaLemon® brand; add water. Cover; chill. Serve over ice.

TIP: This recipe can be doubled.

VARIATIONS

ReaLimeade: Substitute ReaLime® Lime Juice from Concentrate for ReaLemon® brand.

Sparkling: Substitute club soda for cold water.

Slushy: Reduce water to 1/2 cup. In blender container, combine ReaLemon® brand and sugar with 1/2 cup water. Gradually add 4 cups ice cubes, blending until smooth. Serve immediately.

Pink: Stir in 1 to 2 teaspoons grenadine syrup *or* 1 to 2 drops red food coloring.

Minted: Stir in 2 to 3 drops peppermint extract.

Low Calorie: Omit sugar. Add 4 to 8 envelopes sugar substitute *or* 1 1/2 teaspoons liquid sugar substitute.

Strawberry: Increase sugar to 3/4 cup. In blender or food processor, purée 1 quart (about 1 1/2 pounds) fresh strawberries, cleaned and hulled; add to lemonade. (Makes about 2 quarts)

Grape: Stir in 1 (6-ounce) can frozen grape juice concentrate, thawed.

FRESH SALSA PICANTE

Makes about 4 cups

3 firm fresh tomatoes, seeded
   and chopped
1 green bell pepper, chopped
1/2 cup chopped onion or green
   onions
1 Anaheim chili, chopped
2 tablespoons chopped fresh
   cilantro
2 cloves garlic, finely chopped
1 tablespoon ReaLime® Lime
   Juice from Concentrate *or*
   ReaLemon® Lemon Juice
   from Concentrate
1/2 teaspoon chili powder
1/2 teaspoon ground cumin
1/2 teaspoon garlic salt

In medium bowl, combine ingredients; mix well. Cover. Chill. Serve with LaFamous® Tortilla Chips. Refrigerate leftovers.

Clockwise from top right: Minted ReaLemonade, Sparkling ReaLemonade, Slushy ReaLemonade and Pink ReaLemonade

TERIYAKI SCALLOP ROLL-UPS

Makes 2 dozen

12 slices bacon, partially cooked, drained and cut in half crosswise
1/3 cup ReaLime® Lime Juice from Concentrate
1/4 cup soy sauce
1/4 cup vegetable oil
1 tablespoon light brown sugar
2 cloves garlic, finely chopped
1/2 teaspoon pepper
1/2 pound sea scallops, cut in half
24 fresh pea pods
12 water chestnuts, cut in half

In small bowl, combine ReaLime® brand, soy sauce, oil, sugar, garlic and pepper; mix well. Wrap 1 scallop half, 1 pea pod and 1 water chestnut half in each bacon slice; secure with wooden pick. Place in large shallow dish; pour marinade over. Cover; marinate in refrigerator 4 hours or overnight, turning occasionally. Preheat oven to 450°. Remove roll-ups from marinade; discard marinade. Place roll-ups on rack in aluminum foil-lined shallow baking pan; bake 6 minutes. Turn; bake 6 minutes longer or until bacon is crisp. Serve hot. Refrigerate leftovers.

Top to bottom: Teriyaki Scallop Roll-Ups and Teriyaki Chicken Wings

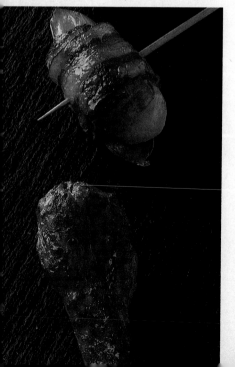

TERIYAKI CHICKEN WINGS

Makes about 3 dozen

1/3 cup ReaLemon® Lemon Juice from Concentrate
1/4 cup ketchup
1/4 cup soy sauce
1/4 cup vegetable oil
2 tablespoons brown sugar
1/4 teaspoon garlic powder
1/4 teaspoon pepper
3 pounds chicken wing drumettes *or* chicken wings, cut at joints and wing tips removed

In large shallow dish or plastic bag, combine all ingredients except chicken; mix well. Add chicken. Cover; marinate in refrigerator 6 hours or overnight, turning occasionally. Preheat oven to 375°. Arrange chicken on rack in aluminum foil-lined shallow baking pan. Bake 40 to 45 minutes. Serve hot. Refrigerate leftovers.

MICROWAVE: Prepare chicken as above. Divide chicken between two 8-inch microwave-safe dishes; pour half of marinade over each. Cover with wax paper; cook each dish on 100% power (high) 12 to 14 minutes or until tender, rearranging pieces once or twice during cooking.

Layered Taco Dip

LAYERED TACO DIP

Makes 12 to 15 servings

1 pound lean ground beef
1 (4-ounce) can chopped green chilies, undrained
2 teaspoons Wyler's® or Steero® Beef-Flavor Instant Bouillon
1 (15- or 16-ounce) can refried beans
1 (16-ounce) container Borden® or Meadow Gold® Sour Cream
1 (1.7-ounce) package taco seasoning mix
Guacamole
Garnishes: Shredded Cheddar or Monterey Jack cheese, chopped fresh tomatoes, sliced green onions, sliced ripe olives
LaFamous® Tortilla Chips

In large skillet, brown beef; pour off fat. Add chilies and bouillon; cook and stir until bouillon dissolves. Cool. Stir in refried beans. In small bowl, combine sour cream and taco seasoning; set aside. In 7- or 8-inch springform pan or on large plate, spread beef mixture. Top with sour cream mixture then guacamole. Cover; chill several hours. Just before serving, remove side of springform pan and garnish as desired. Serve with tortilla chips. Refrigerate leftovers.

Guacamole

In small bowl, mash 3 ripe avocados, pitted and peeled. Add ³/₄ cup chopped fresh tomato, 2 tablespoons ReaLemon® Lemon Juice from Concentrate *or* ReaLime® Lime Juice from Concentrate, ¹/₂ teaspoon seasoned salt and ¹/₈ teaspoon garlic salt; mix well. (Makes about 2 cups)

New England Maple Ribs

PIÑA COLADA

Makes about 7 cups

1¼ cups pineapple juice, chilled
⅔ cup Coco Lopez® Cream of Coconut
1 cup (8 ounces) light rum, optional
5 cups crushed ice

In large blender container, combine ingredients; blend until smooth. Garnish as desired. Serve immediately.

Piña Colada

NEW ENGLAND MAPLE RIBS

Makes 6 to 8 servings

2 pounds spareribs, cut into serving-size pieces
¾ cup Cary's®, MacDonald's™ or Maple Orchards® Pure Maple Syrup
¼ cup Bennett's® Chili Sauce
¼ cup chopped onion
1 tablespoon vinegar
1 tablespoon Worcestershire sauce
1 teaspoon dry mustard
1 clove garlic, finely chopped

In large saucepan or Dutch oven, place ribs; add water to cover. Bring to a boil; cover and simmer 30 minutes or until tender. Drain; refrigerate. In large shallow dish or plastic bag, combine all ingredients except ribs; mix well. Add ribs. Cover; marinate in refrigerator 4 hours or overnight, turning occasionally. Grill or broil ribs as desired, basting frequently with sauce. Discard any remaining sauce. Refrigerate leftovers.

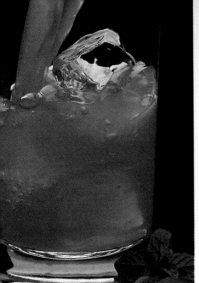
Lemony Iced Tea

LEMONY ICED TEA

Makes about 7 cups

³/₄ cup sugar
**¹/₂ cup ReaLemon® Lemon Juice
  from Concentrate**
6 cups brewed tea
  Ice

In pitcher, dissolve sugar in
ReaLemon® brand; stir until sugar
dissolves. Add tea. Cover; chill.
Serve over ice.

FROZEN MARGARITAS

Makes about 1 quart

¹/₂ cup tequila
**¹/₃ cup ReaLime® Lime Juice from
  Concentrate**
**¹/₄ cup triple sec or other orange-
  flavored liqueur**
1 cup confectioners' sugar
4 cups ice cubes

In blender container, combine all
ingredients except ice; blend well.
Gradually add ice, blending until
smooth. Garnish as desired. Serve
immediately.

LEMONY LIGHT COOLER

Makes about 7 cups

3 cups white grape juice *or*
  **1 (750mL) bottle dry white
    wine, chilled**
¹/₂ to ³/₄ cup sugar
**¹/₂ cup ReaLemon® Lemon Juice
  from Concentrate**
**1 (1-liter) bottle club soda,
  chilled**
  **Strawberries, plum, peach or
    orange slices or other fresh
    fruit**
  Ice

In pitcher, combine grape juice,
sugar and ReaLemon® brand; stir
until sugar dissolves. Cover; chill.
Just before serving, add club soda
and fruit. Serve over ice.

TIP: Recipe can be doubled.

SOUTHERN SUNSHINE

Makes about 7 cups

2 cups orange juice
**¹/₂ cup ReaLemon® Lemon Juice
  from Concentrate**
¹/₄ cup sugar
**4 cups lemon-lime carbonated
  beverage, chilled**
**³/₄ cup Southern Comfort®*
  liqueur, optional**
  Ice

In pitcher, combine juices and
sugar; stir until sugar dissolves.
Cover; chill. Just before serving, add
carbonated beverage and liqueur if
desired. Serve over ice. Garnish as
desired.

TIP: Recipe can be doubled.

**Southern Comfort is a registered
trademark of the Southern Comfort
Corporation.*

Shrimp Cocktail Strata Tart

SHRIMP COCKTAIL STRATA TART

Makes one 10-inch tart

2 1/2 cups fresh bread crumbs (5 slices)
1 cup Borden® or Meadow Gold® Half-and-Half
4 eggs, beaten
2 (4 1/4-ounce) cans Orleans® Shrimp, drained and soaked as label directs
1/2 cup Bennett's® Cocktail *or* Hot Seafood Sauce
1/4 cup chopped green onions
2 tablespoons ReaLemon® Lemon Juice from Concentrate
1 1/2 teaspoons Wyler's® or Steero® Chicken-Flavor Instant Bouillon
1/4 teaspoon pepper
Additional Bennett's® Cocktail *or* Hot Seafood Sauce

Preheat oven to 350°. In large bowl, combine crumbs and half-and-half; let stand 10 minutes. Add remaining ingredients except additional cocktail sauce; mix well. Pour into 10-inch oiled quiche dish or tart pan. Bake 30 to 35 minutes or until set. Cool. Garnish as desired. Serve warm or chilled with additional cocktail sauce. Refrigerate leftovers.

CRAB-STUFFED MUSHROOMS

Makes 12 appetizers

12 large fresh mushrooms
1/4 cup margarine or butter
2 tablespoons finely chopped onion
1 to 4 cloves garlic, finely chopped
1 tablespoon chopped parsley
1/4 cup plain dry bread crumbs or cracker crumbs
1 (6-ounce) can Harris® or Orleans® Crab Meat, drained
Seafood seasoning blend or seasoned salt to taste

Preheat oven to 350°. Remove stems from mushrooms and finely chop. In large skillet, lightly brown mushroom caps in margarine; place in 8- or 9-inch square baking dish. In same skillet, cook chopped mushroom stems, onion, garlic and parsley until lightly browned. Stir in crumbs and crab meat; fill mushroom caps. Bake 8 to 10 minutes or until hot. Serve immediately. Refrigerate leftovers.

BLOODY MARY

Makes about 2 quarts

1 (46-ounce) can tomato juice
1 1/2 cups vodka, optional
3 tablespoons ReaLemon® Lemon Juice from Concentrate
4 teaspoons Worcestershire sauce
1 teaspoon celery salt
1/4 teaspoon hot pepper sauce
1/8 teaspoon pepper

In pitcher, combine ingredients; serve over ice. Garnish as desired.

FRUIT MEDLEY PUNCH

Makes about 3 1/2 quarts

Della Robbia Ice Ring or ice
2 (10-ounce) packages frozen
strawberries in syrup,
thawed
3 cups apricot nectar, chilled
3 cups cold water
1 cup ReaLemon® Lemon Juice
from Concentrate
1 cup sugar
1 (6-ounce) can frozen orange
juice concentrate, thawed
3 (12-ounce) cans ginger ale,
chilled

Prepare ice ring in advance if desired. In blender container, purée strawberries. In large punch bowl, combine puréed strawberries and remaining ingredients except ginger ale and ice ring; stir until sugar dissolves. Just before serving, add ginger ale and ice ring.

Della Robbia Ice Ring

Combine 2 (12-ounce) cans ginger ale (3 cups) and 1/2 cup ReaLemon® brand. Pour 2 1/2 cups mixture into 1-quart ring mold; freeze. Arrange apricot halves, green grapes, strawberries, orange peel strips or other fruits and mint on top of ice. Slowly pour remaining lemon mixture over fruit; freeze.

LEMON ICE CUBES

Makes about 2 dozen

1 quart cold water
1/2 cup ReaLemon® Lemon Juice
from Concentrate
Mint leaves or fruit pieces,
optional

Combine water and ReaLemon® brand. Fill ice cube trays. Place mint leaf or fruit piece in each cube if desired; freeze. Serve with iced tea, lemonade or carbonated beverages.

Fruit Medley Punch

White Sangria

RAINBOW PARTY PUNCH

Makes about 3¹/₂ quarts

**1 (4-serving size) package
 orange, raspberry or lime-
 flavored gelatin
1¹/₂ cups sugar
2 cups boiling water
1 (46-ounce) can pineapple
 juice, chilled
2 cups ReaLemon® Lemon Juice
 from Concentrate
1 quart Borden® or Meadow
 Gold® Orange, Raspberry or
 Lime Sherbet
1 (1-liter) bottle club soda,
 chilled**

In medium bowl, dissolve gelatin
and sugar in water; set aside. In
large bowl, combine pineapple
juice, ReaLemon® brand and
reserved gelatin mixture. Chill. Just
before serving, pour juice mixture
into punch bowl; add sherbet and
club soda.

Rainbow Party Punch

WHITE SANGRIA

Makes about 2 quarts

**³/₄ cup sugar
¹/₂ cup ReaLemon® Lemon Juice
 from Concentrate
¹/₄ cup ReaLime® Lime Juice from
 Concentrate
1 (750 mL) bottle Rhine wine,
 chilled
¹/₃ cup orange-flavored liqueur *or*
 orange juice
1 (1-liter) bottle club soda,
 chilled
Orange, plum or nectarine
 slices, green grapes or other
 fresh fruit
Ice**

In pitcher, combine sugar and
juices; stir until sugar dissolves.
Cover; chill. Just before serving, add
wine, liqueur, club soda and fruit;
serve over ice.

Left to right: Sweet and Sour Meatballs and Creamy Slaw Dip

SWEET AND SOUR MEATBALLS

Makes about 4 dozen

1½ pounds lean ground beef
1 cup fresh bread crumbs
   (2 slices)
1 egg, slightly beaten
4 teaspoons Wyler's® or Steero®
   Beef-Flavor Instant Bouillon
1⅓ cups Bama® Apricot Preserves
2 tablespoons ReaLemon® Lemon
   Juice from Concentrate

In large bowl, combine beef,
crumbs, egg and 2 *teaspoons*
bouillon; mix well. Shape into 1¼-
inch balls. In large skillet, brown
meatballs. Remove from pan; pour
off fat. In same skillet, combine
preserves, ReaLemon® brand and
remaining 2 *teaspoons* bouillon.
Over low heat, cook and stir 10
minutes. Add meatballs; simmer
uncovered 10 minutes. Garnish with
parsley if desired. Refrigerate
leftovers.

CREAMY SLAW DIP

Makes about 1½ cups

1½ cups Borden® or Meadow
   Gold® Sour Cream
1 cup finely shredded cabbage
1 (8-ounce) can water chestnuts,
   drained and finely chopped
⅓ cup prepared slaw dressing
¼ cup chopped green onions
2 teaspoons Wyler's® or Steero®
   Beef-Flavor Instant Bouillon
¼ teaspoon garlic powder

In medium bowl, combine
ingredients; mix well. Cover; chill to
blend flavors. Garnish as desired.
Serve with Krunchers!® Potato Chips
or assorted fresh vegetables.
Refrigerate leftovers.

Soups, Salads & Side Dishes

ORIENTAL CHICKEN SALAD

Makes 4 servings

4 skinned boneless chicken breast halves (about 1 pound)
1/2 cup water
1/3 cup cider vinegar
3 tablespoons vegetable oil
2 tablespoons brown sugar
1 tablespoon soy sauce
2 teaspoons Wyler's® or Steero® Chicken-Flavor Instant Bouillon *or* 2 Chicken-Flavor Bouillon Cubes
Napa (Chinese cabbage)
Alfalfa sprouts, sliced fresh mushrooms, carrot curls and pea pods

In large shallow dish or plastic bag, place chicken. In small saucepan, combine water, vinegar, *1 tablespoon* oil, sugar, soy sauce and bouillon; cook and stir until bouillon dissolves. Cool. Reserving *1/2 cup* dressing; pour remainder over chicken. Cover; marinate in refrigerator 30 minutes. Remove chicken from marinade. In skillet, cook chicken in remaining *2 tablespoons* oil until tender. Cut into thin slices. Line 4 plates with napa. Top with chicken, sprouts, mushrooms, carrots and pea pods. Serve with reserved dressing. Refrigerate leftovers.

NEW ENGLAND CLAM CHOWDER

Makes about 5 cups

3 tablespoons diced salt pork *or* 3 slices bacon
1/4 cup finely chopped onion
2 to 4 tablespoons flour, optional
2 cups pared diced potatoes
1 (8-ounce) bottle Doxsee® or Snow's® Clam Juice
2 (6½-ounce) cans Doxsee® or Snow's® Chopped Clams, drained, reserving liquid
1/8 teaspoon thyme leaves
1½ cups Borden® or Meadow Gold® Half-and-Half

In medium saucepan, brown pork. Add onion; cook until tender. Stir in desired amount of flour until blended; add potatoes, clam juice, reserved clam liquid and thyme. Cover; simmer 10 to 15 minutes or until potatoes are tender. Add half-and-half and clams; heat through (*do not boil*). Refrigerate leftovers.

Oriental Chicken Salad

Left to right: Chicken Corn Chowder and Texas-Style Chili

CHICKEN CORN CHOWDER

Makes about 1³/4 quarts

1¹/₂ cups cubed cooked chicken or
    turkey
4 slices bacon
¹/₂ cup chopped onion
¹/₂ teaspoon thyme leaves
3 tablespoons flour
3 cups Borden® or Meadow
    Gold® Half-and-Half *or* Milk
2 cups water
1 (10-ounce) package frozen
    whole kernel corn
1 medium potato, pared and
    diced
2 tablespoons Wyler's® or
    Steero® Chicken-Flavor
    Instant Bouillon *or*
    6 Chicken-Flavor Bouillon
    Cubes
¹/₄ teaspoon pepper

In large saucepan, cook bacon until crisp; remove and crumble. In drippings, cook onion and thyme until tender; stir in flour until blended. Add chicken and remaining ingredients except bacon; bring to a boil. Reduce heat; simmer 30 minutes or until vegetables are tender, stirring occasionally. Garnish with bacon. Refrigerate leftovers.

TIP: 2 (5- or 6³/4-ounce) cans chunk chicken can be substituted for cooked chicken; add during last 10 minutes of cooking time.

TEXAS-STYLE CHILI

Makes about 4 quarts

3 pounds boneless stew beef, cut
 into ½-inch cubes *or*
 3 pounds lean ground beef
1½ cups chopped onion
1 cup chopped green bell
 pepper
3 cloves garlic, chopped
2 (28-ounce) cans whole
 tomatoes, undrained and
 broken up
2 cups water
1 (6-ounce) can tomato paste
8 teaspoons Wyler's® or Steero®
 Beef-Flavor Instant Bouillon
 or 8 Beef-Flavor Bouillon
 Cubes
2 tablespoons chili powder
1 tablespoon ground cumin
2 teaspoons oregano leaves
2 teaspoons sugar

In large kettle or Dutch oven, brown
beef (if using ground beef, pour off
fat). Add onion, green pepper and
garlic; cook and stir until tender.
Add remaining ingredients. Cover;
bring to a boil. Reduce heat; simmer
1½ hours (1 hour for ground beef)
or until meat is tender, stirring
occasionally. Serve with LaFamous®
Tortilla Chips and shredded cheese if
desired. Refrigerate leftovers.

SPICY MONTEREY RICE

Makes 6 servings

2 cups water
1 cup uncooked long grain rice
1 tablespoon Wyler's® or Steero®
 Chicken-Flavor Instant
 Bouillon *or* 3 Chicken-Flavor
 Bouillon Cubes
1 (16-ounce) container Borden®
 or Meadow Gold® Sour
 Cream, at room temperature
1½ cups (6 ounces) shredded
 Colby cheese
1 cup (4 ounces) shredded
 Monterey Jack cheese
1 (4-ounce) can chopped green
 chilies, undrained
½ cup chopped red bell pepper
⅛ teaspoon pepper

Preheat oven to 350°. In medium
saucepan, combine water, rice and
bouillon; bring to a boil. Reduce
heat; cover and simmer 15 minutes
or until rice is tender. In large bowl,
combine all ingredients except ½
cup Colby cheese; mix well. Turn
into buttered 1½-quart baking dish.
Bake 20 to 25 minutes. Top with
remaining ½ *cup* Colby cheese;
bake 3 minutes longer or until
cheese melts. Let stand 5 minutes.
Garnish as desired. Refrigerate
leftovers.

Spicy Monterey Rice

Broccoli Cheese Soup

BROCCOLI CHEESE SOUP

Makes about 2 quarts

½ cup chopped onion
¼ cup margarine or butter
¼ cup unsifted flour
3 cups water
2 (10-ounce) packages frozen
  chopped broccoli, thawed
  and well drained
4 teaspoons Wyler's® or Steero®
  Chicken-Flavor Instant
  Bouillon *or* 4 Chicken-Flavor
  Bouillon Cubes
1 teaspoon Worcestershire sauce
3 cups (12 ounces) shredded
  Cheddar cheese
2 cups (1 pint) Borden® or
  Meadow Gold® Coffee
  Cream *or* Half-and-Half

In large kettle or Dutch oven, cook onion in margarine until tender; stir in flour until blended. Gradually add water then broccoli, bouillon and Worcestershire. Over medium heat, cook and stir until thickened and broccoli is tender, about 10 minutes. Add cheese and cream.

Cook and stir until cheese melts and soup is hot (*do not boil*). Garnish as desired. Refrigerate leftovers.

TIP: 6 cups (about 1¼ pounds) chopped fresh broccoli can be substituted for frozen broccoli.

MICROWAVE: In 3- to 4-quart round baking dish, combine onion and margarine; cook covered on 100% power (high) 2 to 3 minutes or until onion is tender. Stir in flour. Gradually stir in water then broccoli, bouillon and Worcestershire. Cook covered on 100% power (high) 10 to 12 minutes or until thickened and broccoli is tender. Add cheese and cream; mix well. Cook covered on 100% power (high) 2 to 4 minutes or until hot.

MARINATED CONFETTI COLESLAW

Makes 6 to 8 servings

5 cups coarsely shredded
  cabbage (about 1 pound)
1 firm fresh tomato, seeded and
  diced
½ cup chopped green bell
  pepper
⅓ cup sliced green onions
½ cup ReaLemon® Lemon Juice
  from Concentrate
⅓ cup sugar
⅓ cup vegetable oil
1 teaspoon salt
½ teaspoon dry mustard

In medium bowl, combine cabbage, tomato, green pepper and green onions. In small saucepan, combine remaining ingredients; bring to a boil. Pour over vegetables. Cover; chill 4 hours or overnight to blend flavors. Refrigerate leftovers.

BACON & EGG POTATO SALAD

Makes 10 to 12 servings

2 pounds potatoes, cooked, peeled and cubed (about 5 cups)
¼ cup sliced green onions
⅓ cup ReaLemon® Lemon Juice from Concentrate
⅓ cup water
¼ cup vegetable oil
1½ teaspoons celery salt
1 teaspoon Worcestershire sauce
½ teaspoon dry mustard
¼ teaspoon pepper
4 slices bacon, cooked, drained and crumbled
3 hard-cooked eggs, chopped
¼ cup grated Parmesan cheese
3 tablespoons chopped parsley

In large bowl, combine potatoes and green onions. In small saucepan, combine ReaLemon® brand, water, oil and seasonings; bring to a boil. Pour over potato mixture; mix well. Cover; chill overnight to blend flavors. Remove from refrigerator 30 minutes before serving; stir in remaining ingredients. Refrigerate leftovers.

Linguine Tuna Salad

LINGUINE TUNA SALAD

Makes 6 servings

½ (1 pound) package Creamette® Linguine, broken in half, cooked as package directs and drained
¼ cup ReaLemon® Lemon Juice from Concentrate *or* ReaLime® Lime Juice from Concentrate
¼ cup vegetable oil
¼ cup sliced green onions
2 teaspoons sugar
1 teaspoon Italian seasoning
1 teaspoon seasoned salt
1 (12½-ounce) can tuna, drained
1 (10-ounce) package frozen green peas, thawed
2 firm fresh tomatoes, seeded and chopped

In large bowl, combine ReaLemon® brand, oil, green onions and seasonings; mix well. Add *hot* linguine; toss. Add remaining ingredients; mix well. Cover; chill. Serve on lettuce if desired. Refrigerate leftovers.

Bacon & Egg Potato Salad

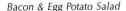

WHITE GAZPACHO

Makes about 1¹/₂ quarts

**3 medium cucumbers, pared,
    seeded and cut into cubes
    (about 3 cups)**
2 cups water
**4 teaspoons Wyler's® or Steero®
    Chicken-Flavor Instant
    Bouillon**
**1 (16-ounce) container Borden®
    or Meadow Gold® Sour
    Cream**
**2 tablespoons ReaLemon® Lemon
    Juice from Concentrate *or*
    ReaLime® Lime Juice from
    Concentrate**
¹/₄ teaspoon garlic powder
¹/₄ teaspoon pepper

In blender or food processor
container, purée cucumbers with *¹/₂
cup* water and bouillon. In medium
bowl, combine cucumber mixture
and remaining ingredients. Chill. Stir
before serving. Garnish as desired.
Serve with condiments. Refrigerate
leftovers.

CONDIMENTS: Chopped fresh
tomato, green onions, green bell
pepper, toasted slivered almonds
and croutons.

White Gazpacho

SEASONED PASTA PILAF

Makes 4 to 6 servings

¹/₂ cup chopped onion
2 cloves garlic, finely chopped
**2 tablespoons margarine or
    butter**
2¹/₂ cups water
1 cup uncooked long grain rice
**1 cup (4 ounces) Creamette®
    Fideos or Vermicelli, broken
    into small pieces**
**1 tablespoon Wyler's® or Steero®
    Chicken-Flavor Instant
    Bouillon *or* 3 Chicken-Flavor
    Bouillon Cubes**
1¹/₂ teaspoons chili powder
¹/₂ teaspoon ground cumin

In large saucepan, cook onion and
garlic in margarine until tender. Add
remaining ingredients; bring to a
boil. Reduce heat; cover and simmer
15 to 20 minutes or until rice is
tender and liquid is absorbed.
Refrigerate leftovers.

HERBED BUTTERMILK DRESSING

Makes about 2 cups

**1 cup Borden® or Meadow
    Gold® Buttermilk**
**1 cup mayonnaise or salad
    dressing**
1 teaspoon basil leaves
¹/₂ teaspoon garlic salt
¹/₂ teaspoon thyme leaves
¹/₄ teaspoon onion powder
¹/₄ teaspoon pepper

In small bowl, combine ingredients;
mix well. Cover; chill to blend
flavors. Serve with salads or as a
vegetable dip. Refrigerate leftovers.

Marinated Oriental Beef Salad

MARINATED ORIENTAL BEEF SALAD

Makes 4 servings

1 (1- to 1¼-pound) beef flank
   steak
⅓ cup ReaLemon® Lemon Juice
   from Concentrate
¼ cup ketchup
¼ cup vegetable oil
1 tablespoon brown sugar
¼ teaspoon garlic powder
¼ teaspoon ground ginger
¼ teaspoon pepper
8 ounces fresh mushrooms,
   sliced (about 2 cups)
1 (8-ounce) can sliced water
   chestnuts, drained
1 medium sweet onion, sliced
   and separated into rings
4 ounces fresh pea pods *or*
   1 (6-ounce) package frozen
   pea pods, thawed

Grill or broil steak 5 minutes on each side or to desired doneness; slice diagonally into thin strips. Meanwhile, in large shallow dish or plastic bag, combine ReaLemon® brand, ketchup, oil, sugar, garlic powder, ginger and pepper; mix well. Add sliced steak, mushrooms, water chestnuts and onion; mix well. Cover; marinate in refrigerator 8 hours or overnight, stirring occasionally. Before serving, add pea pods. Serve on lettuce; garnish with tomato if desired. Refrigerate leftovers.

Savory Lemon Vegetables

SAVORY LEMON VEGETABLES

Makes 8 servings

6 slices bacon, cooked and crumbled, reserving ¼ cup drippings
1 pound carrots, pared and cut into 2-inch pieces
1 medium head cauliflower, core removed
1 cup finely chopped onion
½ cup ReaLemon® Lemon Juice from Concentrate
½ cup water
4 teaspoons sugar
1 teaspoon salt
1 teaspoon thyme leaves
Chopped parsley

In large saucepan, cook carrots and cauliflower in small amount of water until tender. Meanwhile, in medium skillet, cook onion in reserved drippings until tender. Add ReaLemon® brand, ½ cup water, sugar, salt and thyme; bring to a boil. Drain carrots and cauliflower; arrange on serving dish. Pour warm sauce over vegetables. Garnish with bacon and parsley. Refrigerate leftovers.

MICROWAVE: Cook bacon, reserving ¼ cup drippings. On large glass platter with rim, arrange cauliflower and carrots. Cover with vented plastic wrap; cook on 100% power (high) 14 to 16 minutes. In 1-quart glass measure with handle, cook reserved drippings and onion on 100% power (high) 1 minute. Add ReaLemon® brand, water, sugar, salt and thyme. Cook on 100% power (high) 5½ to 6 minutes or until sauce boils. Proceed as above.

FRESH CORN SAUTÉ

Makes 4 to 6 servings

4 ears fresh corn
4 ounces fresh pea pods
1 red bell pepper, cut into strips
¼ cup sliced green onions
1½ teaspoons Wyler's® or Steero®
  Chicken-Flavor Instant
  Bouillon
1 teaspoon sugar
2 tablespoons olive or
  vegetable oil
Freshly ground black pepper

Remove husks and silk from corn;
cut corn from cobs. In large skillet,
cook corn, pea pods, red pepper,
green onions, bouillon and sugar in
oil until tender-crisp. Serve with
ground black pepper. Refrigerate
leftovers.

LEMONY LOW-CAL DRESSING

*Makes about 1 cup; 8 calories per
tablespoon*

⅔ cup plus 2 tablespoons water
¼ cup ReaLemon® Lemon Juice
  from Concentrate
1 (1.3-ounce) package low-
  calorie Italian salad
  dressing mix

In 1-pint jar with tight-fitting lid or
cruet, combine ingredients; shake
well. Chill to blend flavors.
Refrigerate leftovers.

*Caloric values by product analyses
and recipe calculation*

PARTY POTATO SALAD

Makes 10 to 12 servings

1 cup Borden® or Meadow
  Gold® Buttermilk
1 cup mayonnaise or salad
  dressing
2 tablespoons prepared
  horseradish
2 teaspoons Wyler's® or Steero®
  Chicken-Flavor Instant
  Bouillon
2 teaspoons sugar
1 teaspoon dill weed
3 pounds tiny new potatoes,
  cooked and sliced (about
  8 cups)
1 pound cooked and peeled
  small shrimp *or* cubed
  cooked ham, optional
1 cup sliced celery
1 cup sliced green onions
8 slices bacon, cooked, drained
  and crumbled

In large bowl, mix buttermilk,
mayonnaise, horseradish, bouillon,
sugar and dill. Stir in remaining
ingredients. Cover; chill. Garnish as
desired. Refrigerate leftovers.

Party Potato Salad

Celery Seed Dressing

In medium saucepan, combine bouillon and water; bring to a boil. Add remaining ingredients; return to a boil. Reduce heat; cover and simmer 15 to 20 minutes or until rice is tender and liquid is absorbed.

CELERY SEED DRESSING

Makes about 1 cup

½ cup sugar
¼ cup ReaLemon® Lemon Juice from Concentrate
2 teaspoons cider vinegar
1 teaspoon dry mustard
½ teaspoon salt
½ cup vegetable oil
1 teaspoon celery seed or poppy seed

In blender or food processor container, combine all ingredients except oil and celery seed; blend until smooth. On low speed, slowly add oil. Stir in celery seed. Cover; chill to blend flavors. Serve with tossed salad or fruit salad. Refrigerate leftovers.

SEASONED RICE

Makes 6 servings

1 tablespoon Wyler's® or Steero® Beef- or Chicken-Flavor Instant Bouillon *or* 3 Beef- or Chicken-Flavor Bouillon Cubes
2 to 2½ cups water
1 cup uncooked long grain rice
1 tablespoon margarine or butter
1 tablespoon chopped parsley

CHICKEN NOODLE SOUP

Makes about 3 quarts

4 cups cubed cooked chicken or turkey
1 cup chopped celery
1 cup chopped onion
¼ cup margarine or butter
9 cups water
1 cup diced carrots
8 teaspoons Wyler's® or Steero® Chicken-Flavor Instant Bouillon *or* 8 Chicken-Flavor Bouillon Cubes
½ teaspoon marjoram leaves
¼ to ½ teaspoon pepper
1 bay leaf
4 ounces (about 2 cups) uncooked Creamette® or Pennsylvania Dutch® Brand Medium Egg Noodles
1 tablespoon chopped parsley

In large kettle or Dutch oven, cook celery and onion in margarine until tender; add water, chicken, carrots, bouillon, marjoram, pepper and bay leaf. Bring to a boil. Reduce heat; cover and simmer 30 minutes. Remove bay leaf; add noodles and parsley. Cook 10 minutes longer or until noodles are tender, stirring occasionally. Refrigerate leftovers.

Marinated Potato & Mushroom Salad

MARINATED POTATO & MUSHROOM SALAD

Makes 4 to 6 servings

1½ pounds small new potatoes, cooked and cubed (about 4 cups)
1 cup sliced fresh mushrooms (about 4 ounces)
⅓ cup sliced celery
¼ cup sliced green onions
⅓ cup vegetable oil
¼ cup ReaLemon® Lemon Juice from Concentrate *or* ReaLime® Lime Juice from Concentrate
1½ teaspoons Dijon-style mustard
1 teaspoon sugar
1 teaspoon Wyler's® or Steero® Chicken-Flavor Instant Bouillon

In large shallow dish, combine potatoes, mushrooms, celery and green onions. In 1-pint jar with tight-fitting lid, combine remaining ingredients; shake well. Pour over potato mixture; mix well. Cover; marinate in refrigerator 3 hours or overnight, stirring occasionally. Refrigerate leftovers.

PASTA & VEGETABLE TOSS

Makes 4 to 6 servings

½ cup chopped onion
1 clove garlic, finely chopped
1 teaspoon Italian seasoning
1 tablespoon olive oil
¼ cup water
2 teaspoons Wyler's® or Steero® Beef-Flavor Instant Bouillon
2 cups fresh broccoli flowerets
2 cups sliced zucchini
8 ounces fresh mushrooms, sliced (about 2 cups)
1 red bell pepper, cut into thin strips
½ (1-pound) package Creamette® Fettuccini, cooked as package directs and drained

In large skillet, cook onion, garlic and Italian seasoning in oil until tender. Add water, bouillon and vegetables. Cover and simmer 5 to 7 minutes until vegetables are tender-crisp. Toss with *hot* fettuccini. Serve immediately. Refrigerate leftovers.

Classic French Onion Soup

MICROWAVE: In 2-quart glass measure with handle, melt margarine on 100% power (high) 1 minute. Add onions and garlic; cook covered on 100% power (high) 5 to 6 minutes or until tender. Add water, sherry and *instant* bouillon. Cook covered on 100% power (high) 8 to 13 minutes or until boiling; stir. Cook on 50% power (medium) 20 minutes to blend flavors. Proceed as directed.

CLASSIC FRENCH ONION SOUP

Makes 6 servings

4 cups thinly sliced sweet onions
1 clove garlic, finely chopped
¼ cup margarine or butter
5½ cups water
⅓ cup dry sherry *or* white wine *or* water
7 teaspoons Wyler's® or Steero® Beef-Flavor Instant Bouillon *or* 7 Beef-Flavor Bouillon Cubes
6 (¾-inch thick) slices French bread, buttered and toasted
6 (8×4-inch) slices Swiss cheese, cut in half crosswise

In large saucepan, cook onions and garlic in margarine until tender. Add water, sherry and bouillon. Bring to a boil; reduce heat. Cover and simmer 30 minutes, stirring occasionally. Ladle into 6 ovenproof soup bowls. Top each serving with a bread slice and 2 pieces of cheese. Broil until cheese melts. Serve immediately. Refrigerate leftovers.

TACO SALAD

Makes 4 servings

1 pound lean ground beef
1 (14½-ounce) can stewed tomatoes, undrained
1 (4-ounce) can chopped green chilies, undrained
2 teaspoons Wyler's® or Steero® Beef-Flavor Instant Bouillon *or* 2 Beef-Flavor Bouillon Cubes
¼ teaspoon hot pepper sauce
⅛ teaspoon garlic powder
Dash pepper
4 cups shredded lettuce (1 medium head)
1 to 1½ cups Wise® Corn Chips or LaFamous® Tortilla Chips
1 firm fresh tomato, seeded and chopped
1 cup (4 ounces) shredded Cheddar cheese

In large skillet, brown beef; pour off fat. Add stewed tomatoes, chilies, bouillon, hot pepper sauce, garlic powder and pepper; simmer uncovered 20 minutes. In large bowl or on platter, arrange lettuce then beef mixture, chips, chopped tomato and cheese. Refrigerate leftovers.

CREAMY FETTUCCINI TOSS

Makes 4 to 6 servings

- ¼ cup margarine or butter
- 1 tablespoon flour
- 2 teaspoons Wyler's® or Steero® Chicken-Flavor Instant Bouillon
- ¾ teaspoon basil leaves
- ¼ teaspoon garlic powder
- ⅛ teaspoon pepper
- 1 cup (½ pint) Borden® or Meadow Gold® Coffee Cream *or* Half-and-Half
- 1 cup Borden® or Meadow Gold® Milk
- ½ (1-pound) package Creamette® Fettuccini
- ¼ cup grated Parmesan cheese Chopped parsley, walnuts and cooked crumbled bacon

In medium saucepan, melt margarine; stir in flour, bouillon, basil, garlic powder and pepper. Gradually add cream and milk. Cook and stir until bouillon dissolves and sauce thickens slightly, about 15 minutes. Meanwhile, cook fettuccini as package directs; drain. Remove sauce from heat; add cheese. In large bowl, pour sauce over *hot* fettuccini; stir to coat. Garnish with parsley, walnuts and bacon. Serve immediately. Refrigerate leftovers.

TROPICAL CHICKEN SALAD

Makes 4 to 6 servings

- 4 cups cubed cooked chicken or turkey
- 2 large oranges, peeled, sectioned and drained
- 1½ cups cut-up fresh pineapple, drained
- 1 cup seedless green grape halves
- 1 cup sliced celery
- ¾ cup mayonnaise or salad dressing
- 3 to 4 tablespoons ReaLemon® Lemon Juice from Concentrate
- ½ teaspoon ground ginger
- ½ teaspoon salt
- ½ to ¾ cup nuts

In large bowl, combine chicken, fruit and celery; mix well. Cover; chill. In small bowl, combine remaining ingredients except nuts. Cover; chill. Just before serving, combine chicken mixture, dressing and nuts. Serve in hollowed-out pineapple shells or on lettuce leaves if desired. Refrigerate leftovers.

Tropical Chicken Salad

Tuna Cobb Salad Pockets

TUNA COBB SALAD POCKETS

Makes 4 sandwiches

⅓ cup vegetable oil
¼ cup ReaLemon® Lemon Juice
  from Concentrate
2 teaspoons red wine vinegar,
  optional
1 teaspoon sugar
½ teaspoon Worcestershire sauce
⅛ teaspoon garlic powder
1 (6½-ounce) can tuna, drained
  and flaked
2 cups shredded lettuce
½ cup diced avocado
½ cup seeded and diced tomato
1 hard-cooked egg, chopped
2 tablespoons cooked crumbled
  bacon
2 tablespoons crumbled blue
  cheese
4 Pita bread rounds, cut in half

In medium bowl, combine oil,
ReaLemon® brand, vinegar and
seasonings; add tuna. Cover;
marinate in refrigerator 1 hour. Stir
in remaining ingredients except Pita
bread. Serve in Pita bread.
Refrigerate leftovers.

BAKED VEGETABLES ITALIANO

Makes 6 to 8 servings

1 cup *each* thinly sliced carrots,
  summer squash, zucchini,
  cauliflowerets and cut green
  beans
1 medium onion, cut into
  wedges
1 firm fresh tomato, cut into
  wedges
½ pound new potatoes, cut into
  wedges (about 1½ cups)
½ cup chopped celery
½ cup thin strips red bell pepper
¼ cup olive or vegetable oil
¼ cup water
1 tablespoon Wyler's® or Steero®
  Chicken-Flavor Instant
  Bouillon
3 cloves garlic, finely chopped
1 teaspoon *each* basil and
  oregano leaves
1 cup shredded Monterey Jack
  cheese
½ cup grated Parmesan cheese

Preheat oven to 350°. Combine
vegetables in 13×9-inch baking dish.
In small saucepan, over low heat,
combine oil, water, bouillon, garlic,
basil and oregano; bring to a boil.
Pour over vegetables. Cover; bake 50
minutes or until tender. Uncover;
top with cheeses. Bake 3 to 5
minutes longer or until cheeses are
melted. Refrigerate leftovers.

HERB CARROT SOUP

Makes about 1¹/₂ quarts

¹/₂ **cup chopped onion**
1 **clove garlic, finely chopped**
2 **tablespoons margarine or
   butter**
1 **pound carrots, pared and
   sliced**
3 **cups water**
1 **tablespoon Wyler's® or Steero®
   Chicken-Flavor Instant
   Bouillon**
1 **teaspoon basil leaves
   Dash pepper**
2 **cups Borden® Lite-line® or
   Viva® Protein Fortified Skim
   Milk**

In large saucepan, cook onion and
garlic in margarine until tender. Add
remaining ingredients except milk;
bring to a boil. Reduce heat; simmer
covered until carrots are tender. In
blender, purée half the carrot
mixture; repeat. In saucepan,
combine milk with carrot purée;
heat through (*do not boil*). Garnish
as desired. Refrigerate leftovers.

Herb Carrot Soup

Light & Easy Cheese Sauce

LIGHT & EASY CHEESE
SAUCE

*Makes about 1³/₄ cups, 18 calories per
tablespoon*

1 **(8-ounce) package Borden®
   Lite-line® Process Cheese
   Product*, any flavor, each
   slice cut into quarters**
1 **cup Borden® Lite-line® or
   Viva® Protein Fortified Skim
   Milk**
   Cayenne pepper, optional

In medium saucepan, combine
ingredients. Over medium heat,
cook and stir until cheese product
melts. Serve warm over fresh or
steamed vegetables, pasta, baked
potatoes or LaFamous® Tortilla
Chips.

**"¹/₂ the calories" — 8% milkfat
product
Caloric values by product analyses
and recipe calculation*

Main Dishes

BEEF, PORK & PASTA

LAYERED PASTA RICOTTA PIE

Makes 6 to 8 servings

1/4 (1-pound) package Creamette®
Vermicelli
1/3 cup finely chopped onion
4 cloves garlic, finely chopped
1 tablespoon olive or
vegetable oil
1 cup grated fresh Romano
cheese
3 eggs
1 (15- or 16-ounce) container
ricotta cheese
1 (10-ounce) package frozen
chopped spinach, thawed
and *well drained*
1/2 teaspoon salt
1 (26-ounce) jar Classico® Di
Sicilia (Ripe Olives &
Mushrooms) Pasta Sauce

Preheat oven to 350°. Break
vermicelli into thirds; cook
according to package directions.
Drain. Meanwhile, in large skillet,
cook onion and garlic in oil until
tender; remove from heat. Add
cooked vermicelli, *1/2 cup* Romano
cheese and *1 egg*; mix well. Press
into well-greased 9-inch springform
pan. Combine *2 egg yolks*, ricotta,
spinach, salt and remaining *1/2 cup*
Romano cheese. Spread over pasta
layer. In small mixer bowl, beat *2*
egg *whites* until stiff but not dry;
fold into *1 1/2 cups* pasta sauce. Pour
over spinach mixture. Bake 50 to 60
minutes or until set; let stand 10
minutes. Heat remaining pasta
sauce; serve with pie. Garnish as
desired. Refrigerate leftovers.

MARINATED FLANK STEAK

Makes 4 to 6 servings

1/2 cup ReaLemon® Lemon Juice
from Concentrate
1/4 cup vegetable oil
2 teaspoons Wyler's® or Steero®
Beef-Flavor Instant Bouillon
2 cloves garlic, finely chopped
1 teaspoon ground ginger
1 (1- to 1 1/2-pound) beef flank
steak

In large shallow dish or plastic bag,
combine ReaLemon® brand, oil,
bouillon, garlic and ginger; add
steak. Cover; marinate in refrigerator
4 to 6 hours, turning occasionally.
Remove steak from marinade; heat
marinade thoroughly. Grill or broil
steak 5 to 7 minutes on each side or
to desired doneness, basting
frequently with marinade. Serve
immediately. Refrigerate leftovers.

Layered Pasta Ricotta Pie

VEAL CUTLETS PARMA STYLE

Makes 4 servings

- ½ (1-pound) package Creamette® Linguine, cooked as package directs and drained
- 2 eggs
- 2 tablespoons water
- ½ teaspoon garlic salt
- 2 cups plain dry bread crumbs
- ½ cup butter or margarine
- 2 tablespoons olive oil
- 8 thin veal cutlets (about 1 pound)
- 1 (26-ounce) jar Classico® Di Sicilia (Ripe Olives & Mushrooms) *or* Di Parma (Four Cheese) Pasta Sauce
- Grated Parmesan cheese

In medium bowl, beat eggs, water and garlic salt. Dip veal in crumbs then in egg mixture and again in crumbs. In large skillet, over medium heat, melt butter with oil; brown veal on both sides. In medium saucepan, heat pasta sauce. Arrange veal on *hot* linguine; top with pasta sauce. Garnish with Parmesan cheese. Refrigerate leftovers.

Veal Cutlets Parma Style

HONEY MUSTARD PORK TENDERLOIN

Makes 2 to 4 servings

- ¼ cup vegetable oil
- 2 tablespoons brown sugar
- 2 tablespoons honey
- 2 tablespoons ReaLemon® Lemon Juice from Concentrate
- 1 tablespoon Dijon-style mustard
- 2 teaspoons Wyler's® or Steero® Beef- *or* Chicken-Flavor Instant Bouillon
- 1 (¾- to 1-pound) pork tenderloin

In shallow dish or plastic bag combine all ingredients except tenderloin; mix well. Add meat. Cover; marinate in refrigerator 6 hours or overnight. Remove tenderloin from marinade; heat marinade thoroughly. Grill or broil tenderloin 30 to 35 minutes or until meat thermometer inserted in center reaches 160°, basting frequently with marinade. Refrigerate leftovers.

CONEY DOG PIE

Makes 6 to 8 servings

- 1 (6½- or 8½-ounce) package corn muffin mix
- 1 pound lean ground beef
- 1 (12-ounce) jar Bennett's® Chili Sauce
- 1 teaspoon Wyler's® or Steero® Beef-Flavor Instant Bouillon
- 1 teaspoon prepared mustard
- 1 pound frankfurters, cut into quarters

Preheat oven to 350°. Prepare muffin mix as package directs. In 12-inch ovenproof skillet, brown beef; pour off fat. Add chili sauce, bouillon, mustard and frankfurters; bring to a boil. Top with prepared corn muffin batter. Bake 20 minutes or until golden brown. Refrigerate leftovers.

Clockwise from top right: Mexican Burger, Italian Burger, Garden Burger and Oriental Burger

SEASONED BURGERS

Makes 4 servings

1½ pounds lean ground beef
**1½ teaspoons Wyler's® or Steero®
Beef-Flavor Instant Bouillon**

Combine ingredients; shape into patties. Grill or broil 5 to 7 minutes on each side or until beef is cooked to desired doneness. Garnish as desired. Refrigerate leftovers.

VARIATIONS

Italian Burgers: Combine beef mixture with 2 tablespoons grated Parmesan cheese and 1 teaspoon Italian seasoning. Cook as directed. Serve with pizza sauce. Garnish as desired.

Oriental Burgers: Combine beef mixture with 1 (8-ounce) can water chestnuts, drained and chopped, and ¼ cup sliced green onions. Cook as directed. Top with pineapple slice; serve with Bennett's® Sweet & Sour Sauce. Garnish as desired.

Mexican Burgers: Combine beef mixture with 1 (4-ounce) can chopped green chilies, drained, and ¼ cup chopped onion. Cook as directed. Serve with Borden® or Meadow Gold® Sour Cream and salsa.

German Burgers: Combine beef mixture with 2 tablespoons chopped dill pickle and 1 teaspoon caraway seed. Cook as directed. Serve with sauerkraut.

Garden Burgers: Combine beef mixture with 1 tablespoon chopped green bell pepper and 2 tablespoons thousand island dressing. Cook as directed. Serve with cole slaw and chopped tomato.

Mandarin Pork Chops with Seasoned Rice (page 22)

MANDARIN PORK CHOPS

Makes 4 servings

4 pork chops (about 1½ pounds)
1 tablespoon vegetable oil
½ cup orange juice
¼ cup water
3 tablespoons brown sugar
2 tablespoons ReaLemon® Lemon Juice from Concentrate
1 tablespoon cornstarch
2 teaspoons Wyler's® or Steero® Chicken-Flavor Instant Bouillon
1 (11-ounce) can mandarin orange segments, drained
1 green bell pepper, sliced

In large skillet, brown pork chops in oil; remove from pan. In same skillet, add juice, water, sugar, ReaLemon® brand, cornstarch and bouillon; cook and stir until slightly thickened. Add pork chops; cover and simmer 20 minutes or until tender. Add orange segments and green pepper; heat through. Refrigerate leftovers.

MOSTACCIOLI AND SAUSAGE

Makes 6 to 8 servings

1½ pounds link Italian sausage, sliced
1 cup chopped onion
¾ cup chopped green bell pepper
2 (26-ounce) jars Classico® Pasta Sauce, any flavor
½ cup grated Parmesan cheese
1 (1-pound) package Creamette® Mostaccioli, cooked as package directs and drained
2 tablespoons olive oil

In large saucepan, brown sausage; pour off fat. Add onion and green pepper; cook and stir until tender. Add pasta sauce and Parmesan cheese. Bring to a boil; reduce heat. Cover and simmer 15 minutes, stirring occasionally. Toss hot cooked mostaccioli with oil. Serve with sauce. Garnish as desired. Refrigerate leftovers.

SPAGHETTI & MEATBALLS

Makes 6 to 8 servings

1 pound lean ground beef
3/4 cup grated Parmesan cheese
1/2 cup finely chopped onion
1/2 cup fresh bread crumbs
   (1 slice)
1 (26-ounce) jar Classico® Pasta
   Sauce, any flavor
1 egg
2 teaspoons Wyler's® or Steero®
   Beef-Flavor Instant Bouillon
1 teaspoon Italian seasoning
8 ounces fresh mushrooms,
   sliced (about 2 cups)
1 (1-pound) package Creamette®
   Spaghetti, cooked as
   package directs and drained

In large bowl, combine beef, cheese, onion, crumbs, *1/2 cup* pasta sauce, egg, bouillon and Italian seasoning; mix well. Shape into balls. In large kettle or Dutch oven, brown meatballs; pour off fat. Stir in remaining pasta sauce and mushrooms; simmer uncovered 10 minutes or until hot. Serve over *hot* cooked spaghetti. Refrigerate leftovers.

Spaghetti & Meatballs

Cheesy Meatloaf

CHEESY MEATLOAF

Makes 6 to 8 servings

1 1/2 pounds lean ground beef
2 cups fresh bread crumbs
   (4 slices)
1 cup tomato juice
1/3 cup chopped onion
2 eggs
2 teaspoons Wyler's® or Steero®
   Beef-Flavor Instant Bouillon
1/4 teaspoon pepper
6 slices Borden® Process
   American Cheese Food

In large bowl, combine all ingredients except cheese food. In shallow baking dish, shape half the meat mixture into loaf. Cut *4 slices* cheese food into strips; arrange on meat. Top with remaining meat mixture; press edges together to seal. Bake at 350° for 1 hour or until set; pour off fat. Top with remaining *2 slices* cheese food. Refrigerate leftovers.

Classic Stuffed Shells

individual ramekins, pour about half the sauce mixture; arrange stuffed shells in sauce. Top with remaining sauce; cover. Bake in preheated 350° oven 30 minutes. Uncover; sprinkle with remaining *1 cup* mozzarella. Bake 3 minutes longer. Refrigerate leftovers.

CLASSIC STUFFED SHELLS

Makes 6 to 8 servings

- 18 Creamette® Jumbo Macaroni Shells, cooked as package directs and drained
- ½ pound lean ground beef
- ⅔ cup chopped onion
- 1 clove garlic, chopped
- 1 (26-ounce) jar Classico® Di Napoli (Tomato & Basil) Pasta Sauce
- 1½ teaspoons oregano leaves
- 1 teaspoon Wyler's® or Steero® Beef-Flavor Instant Bouillon
- 1 (16-ounce) container Borden® or Meadow Gold® Cottage Cheese
- 2 cups (8 ounces) shredded mozzarella cheese
- ½ cup grated Parmesan cheese
- 1 egg

In large skillet, brown beef, onion and garlic; pour off fat. Stir in pasta sauce, oregano and bouillon; simmer 10 minutes. In large bowl, mix cottage cheese, *1 cup* mozzarella, Parmesan cheese and egg. Stuff shells with cheese mixture. In 13×9-inch baking dish or

SLOPPY JOES

Makes 4 to 6 sandwiches

- 1 pound lean ground beef
- 1 (12-ounce) bottle Bennett's® Chili Sauce
- 1 teaspoon Wyler's® or Steero® Beef-Flavor Instant Bouillon
- 1 teaspoon prepared mustard
- 1 teaspoon vinegar
- 4 to 6 hamburger buns, split and toasted

In large skillet, brown beef; pour off fat. Add chili sauce, bouillon, mustard and vinegar; bring to a boil. Reduce heat; cover and simmer 15 minutes. Serve on buns. Refrigerate leftovers.

Sloppy Joes

Beef Fajitas

BEEF FAJITAS

Makes 10 fajitas

½ cup **ReaLemon® Lemon Juice
    from Concentrate *or*
    ReaLime® Lime Juice from
    Concentrate**
¼ cup **vegetable oil**
2 cloves **garlic, finely chopped**
2 teaspoons **Wyler's® or Steero®
    Beef-Flavor Instant Bouillon**
1 (1- to 1½-pound) **top round
    steak**
10 (6-inch) **flour tortillas, warmed
    Garnishes: Picante sauce,
    shredded lettuce, shredded
    Cheddar cheese, sliced green
    onions, sliced ripe olives and
    sour cream**

In large shallow dish or plastic bag, combine ReaLemon® brand, oil, garlic and bouillon; add steak. Cover; marinate in refrigerator 6 hours or overnight. Remove steak from marinade; heat marinade thoroughly. Grill or broil meat 8 to 10 minutes on each side or to desired doneness, basting frequently with marinade. Slice meat diagonally into thin strips; place on tortillas. Top with one or more garnishes; fold tortillas. Serve immediately. Refrigerate leftovers.

Savory Pork Chops & Stuffing

SAVORY PORK CHOPS & STUFFING

Makes 4 servings

- ⅓ cup uncooked wild rice
- 3 teaspoons Wyler's® or Steero® Chicken-Flavor Instant Bouillon
- 4 pork chops (about 1½ pounds)
- ¼ cup margarine or butter
- 1 cup sliced fresh mushrooms (about 4 ounces)
- ⅓ cup chopped celery
- ⅓ cup chopped onion
- ⅓ cup chopped pecans
- 2 cups herb-seasoned stuffing mix
- ⅓ cup water
- ½ teaspoon poultry seasoning

Cook wild rice according to package directions, adding *2 teaspoons* bouillon to water. In large skillet, brown pork chops in margarine; remove pork chops from pan. Add mushrooms, celery, onion and pecans; cook until tender. In large bowl, combine wild rice, vegetable mixture, stuffing mix, water, remaining *1 teaspoon* bouillon and poultry seasoning; mix well. Place stuffing in greased baking dish; top with pork chops. Cover; bake at 350° for 55 to 60 minutes *or* until pork chops are tender. Refrigerate leftovers.

STEAK DI SICILIA

Makes 4 servings

- 2 tablespoons olive or vegetable oil
- 1½ cups fresh bread crumbs (3 slices)
- 1 clove garlic, finely chopped
- 1 teaspoon oregano leaves
- 1¼ cups Classico® Di Sicilia (Ripe Olives & Mushrooms) Pasta Sauce
- ¼ cup grated fresh Parmesan cheese
- 4 to 6 anchovy fillets, drained and chopped
- 4 (4- to 6-ounce) beef tenderloin filets, lightly seasoned with salt and pepper

In large skillet, heat *1 tablespoon* oil; add crumbs, garlic and oregano. Over medium-high heat, cook and stir until crumbs are golden. In medium bowl, combine crumb mixture, pasta sauce, cheese and anchovies; mix well. In same skillet, heat remaining *1 tablespoon* oil. Over medium-high heat, brown filets on both sides; reduce heat. Top each filet with one-fourth crumb mixture; cover. Cook 5 minutes or until heated through and filets are desired doneness. Refrigerate leftovers.

NEAPOLITAN LASAGNA

Makes 9 to 12 servings

1 pound lean ground beef
2 tablespoons olive or
   vegetable oil
2 cups sliced zucchini (about
   ½ pound)
1 cup chopped onion
2 cloves garlic, finely chopped
1 (26-ounce) jar Classico® Di
   Napoli (Tomato & Basil) *or*
   Di Parma (Four Cheese)
   Pasta Sauce
1 tablespoon Wyler's® or Steero®
   Beef-Flavor Instant Bouillon
2 teaspoons oregano leaves
½ teaspoon sugar
1 (16-ounce) container Borden®
   or Meadow Gold® Small
   Curd Cottage Cheese
3 cups (12 ounces) shredded
   mozzarella cheese
2 eggs
¼ cup grated Parmesan cheese
¼ cup unsifted flour
½ (1-pound) package Creamette®
   Lasagna, cooked as package
   directs and drained
   Parsley flakes

In large saucepan, brown beef in oil.
Add zucchini, onion and garlic;
cook until tender. Add pasta sauce,
bouillon, oregano and sugar; simmer
uncovered 20 minutes. Meanwhile,
in medium bowl, combine cottage
cheese, *1 cup* mozzarella, eggs,
Parmesan and flour; mix well. In
13×9-inch baking dish, layer half
each of the lasagna and meat
mixture, all the cottage cheese
mixture and *1 cup* mozzarella.
Repeat layers with remaining lasagna
and meat mixture. Top with *1 cup*
mozzarella; sprinkle with parsley.

Cover; bake in preheated 350° oven
35 to 40 minutes or until bubbly.
Uncover. Let stand 10 minutes before
serving. Refrigerate leftovers.

SOY MARINADE

Makes about 1½ cups

½ cup ReaLemon® Lemon Juice
   from Concentrate
½ cup soy sauce
½ cup vegetable oil
3 tablespoons ketchup
3 to 4 cloves garlic, finely
   chopped
¼ teaspoon pepper

In large shallow dish or plastic bag,
combine ingredients; add beef,
chicken or pork. Cover; marinate in
refrigerator 4 hours or overnight,
turning occasionally. Remove meat
from marinade; heat marinade
thoroughly. Grill or broil meat as
desired, basting frequently with
marinade. Refrigerate leftovers.

Soy Marinated Steak

POULTRY

QUICK CHICKEN CACCIATORE

Makes 4 servings

4 skinned boneless chicken breast halves (about 1 pound)
Salt and pepper
Flour
2 cloves garlic, finely chopped
4 tablespoons olive oil
1 (26-ounce) jar Classico® Di Napoli (Tomato & Basil) *or* Di Sicilia (Ripe Olives & Mushrooms) Pasta Sauce
1 small green bell pepper, cut into thin strips
1 small red bell pepper, cut into thin strips
2 slices Provolone cheese, cut in half
1 (7-ounce) package *or* 2 cups uncooked Creamettes® Elbow Macaroni, cooked as package directs and drained
Chopped parsley

Season chicken with salt and pepper; coat with flour. In large skillet, brown chicken and garlic in *3 tablespoons* oil; remove chicken from pan. Add pasta sauce then chicken. Bring to a boil; reduce heat. Cover and simmer 20 minutes, adding peppers during last 5 minutes. Uncover; top each chicken breast with half cheese slice. Toss hot cooked macaroni with remaining *1 tablespoon* oil and parsley. Serve with chicken and sauce. Refrigerate leftovers.

JALAPEÑO-GLAZED TURKEY BREAST

Makes 6 servings

1 (4- to 4½-pound) fresh bone-in turkey breast half
½ cup water
2 teaspoons cornstarch
2 teaspoons Wyler's® or Steero® Chicken-Flavor Instant Bouillon
¼ cup jalapeño jelly *or* apple jelly
1 tablespoon finely chopped fresh cilantro
2 cloves garlic, finely chopped
½ teaspoon ground cumin
¼ teaspoon red pepper flakes, optional

Grill or roast turkey according to manufacturer's directions, 45 minutes to 2 hours or until meat thermometer reaches 170°. In small saucepan, combine water, cornstarch and bouillon; stir in remaining ingredients. Over medium heat, cook and stir until slightly thickened. Brush turkey with 2 tablespoons sauce during last 5 to 10 minutes of cooking. Serve turkey with remaining sauce. Refrigerate leftovers.

Jalapeño-Glazed Turkey Breast

Southern Fried Chicken Strips

SOUTHERN FRIED CHICKEN STRIPS

Makes 4 servings

1 pound skinned boneless
  chicken breasts, cut into
  strips
3/4 cup Borden® or Meadow
  Gold® Buttermilk
1 tablespoon Wyler's® or Steero®
  Chicken-Flavor Instant
  Bouillon
1/2 teaspoon oregano leaves
1 1/4 cups unsifted flour
1 to 2 teaspoons paprika
  Vegetable oil

In large bowl, combine buttermilk,
bouillon and oregano; let stand 10
minutes. Stir. Add chicken, stirring to
coat. Let stand 30 minutes in
refrigerator to blend flavors. In
plastic bag, combine flour and
paprika. Add chicken, a few pieces
at a time to flour mixture; shake to
coat. Dip in buttermilk mixture
again; coat with flour again. In large
skillet, fry chicken strips in hot oil
until golden on both sides. Drain on
paper towels. Serve with Peach
Dipping Sauce. Refrigerate leftovers.

Peach Dipping Sauce

In blender container, combine 1
(16-ounce) jar Bama® Peach *or*
Apricot Preserves (1 1/2 cups), 1/4 cup
Dijon-style mustard and 2
tablespoons ReaLemon® Lemon
Juice from Concentrate; blend until
smooth. (Makes about 2 cups)

ZESTY TURKEY BURGERS

Makes 4 servings

1 pound ground fresh turkey
1/4 cup Bennett's® Chili Sauce
1 teaspoon Wyler's® or Steero®
  Chicken-Flavor Instant
  Bouillon

Combine ingredients; shape into
patties. Grill, broil or pan-fry until
turkey is no longer pink. Serve with
additional chili sauce if desired.
Refrigerate leftovers.

Zesty Turkey Burgers

Special Lemony Chicken

SPECIAL LEMONY CHICKEN

Makes 6 servings

¼ cup unsifted flour
1 teaspoon Wyler's® or Steero® Chicken-Flavor Instant Bouillon
¼ teaspoon pepper
6 skinned boneless chicken breast halves (about 1½ pounds)
¼ cup margarine or butter
¼ cup ReaLemon® Lemon Juice from Concentrate
8 ounces fresh mushrooms, sliced (about 2 cups)
Hot cooked rice
Chopped parsley

In plastic bag, combine flour, bouillon and pepper. Add chicken, a few pieces at a time; shake to coat. In large skillet, brown chicken in margarine. Add ReaLemon® brand and mushrooms. Reduce heat; cover and simmer 15 minutes or until tender. Serve with rice; garnish with parsley. Refrigerate leftovers.

VERSATILE CHICKEN

Makes 4 to 6 servings

¾ cup Borden® or Meadow Gold® Buttermilk
1 tablespoon Wyler's® or Steero® Chicken-Flavor Instant Bouillon
½ teaspoon oregano leaves, optional
3 pounds chicken pieces
1 cup unsifted flour
1 teaspoon paprika
¼ cup margarine or butter, melted

In large bowl, combine buttermilk, bouillon and oregano; let stand 10 minutes. Stir. Add chicken, stirring to coat. Let stand 30 minutes in refrigerator to blend flavors. In plastic bag, combine flour and paprika. Add chicken, a few pieces at a time to flour mixture; shake to coat. Place in greased 13×9-inch baking dish. Drizzle with margarine. Bake at 350° for 1 hour or until golden. Refrigerate leftovers.

TIP: To fry chicken, omit melted margarine; fry in vegetable oil.

Chicken Parisian with Creamy Fettuccini Toss (page 25)

CHICKEN PARISIAN

Makes 6 servings

1/4 cup unsifted flour
1/4 teaspoon paprika
1/4 teaspoon pepper
6 skinned boneless chicken
     breast halves (about
     1 1/2 pounds)
3 tablespoons margarine or
     butter
8 ounces fresh mushrooms,
     sliced (about 2 cups)
1/2 cup water
1/4 cup dry white wine
2 teaspoons Wyler's® or Steero®
     Chicken-Flavor Instant
     Bouillon *or* 2 Chicken-Flavor
     Bouillon Cubes
2 teaspoons chopped parsley
1/4 teaspoon thyme leaves

In plastic bag, combine flour,
paprika and pepper. Add chicken, a
few pieces at a time; shake to coat.
In skillet, brown chicken in
margarine; remove from pan. In
same skillet, add remaining
ingredients; simmer 3 minutes. Add
chicken; simmer covered 20 minutes
or until tender. Refrigerate leftovers.

CORN BREAD SAUSAGE STUFFING

Makes about 3 quarts

1 pound fresh mushrooms, sliced
     (about 4 cups)
1 cup chopped celery
3/4 cup chopped onion
1/2 cup margarine or butter
4 teaspoons Wyler's® or Steero®
     Chicken-Flavor Instant
     Bouillon *or* 4 Chicken-Flavor
     Bouillon Cubes
1 2/3 cups boiling water
1 pound bulk sausage, browned
     and drained
1 (16-ounce) package corn bread
     stuffing mix
1 1/2 teaspoons poultry seasoning

In large skillet, cook mushrooms,
celery and onion in margarine until
tender. In large bowl, dissolve
bouillon in water. Add sausage,
mushroom mixture and remaining
ingredients; mix well. Loosely stuff
turkey just before roasting if desired.
Place remaining stuffing in greased
baking dish. Bake at 350° for 30
minutes or until hot. Refrigerate
leftovers.

APPLE & HERB STUFFING

Makes about 2½ quarts

- **2 cups sliced celery**
- **1½ cups chopped onion**
- **½ cup margarine or butter**
- **1¾ cups water**
- **1 tablespoon Wyler's® or Steero® Chicken-Flavor Instant Bouillon *or* 3 Chicken-Flavor Bouillon Cubes**
- **12 cups dry bread cubes (about 16 slices)**
- **3 cups coarsely chopped apple**
- **1 cup slivered almonds, toasted**
- **1 tablespoon chopped parsley**
- **2 teaspoons poultry seasoning**
- **¼ teaspoon rubbed sage**

In large skillet, cook celery and onion in margarine until tender. Add water and bouillon; cook until bouillon dissolves. In large bowl, combine remaining ingredients; add bouillon mixture. Mix well. Loosely stuff turkey just before roasting if desired. Place remaining stuffing in greased baking dish. Bake at 350° for 30 minutes or until hot. Serve with Rich Turkey Gravy if desired. Refrigerate leftovers.

Rich Turkey Gravy

In medium skillet, stir ¼ to ⅓ cup flour into ¼ cup pan drippings; cook and stir until dark brown. Stir in 2 cups hot water and 2 teaspoons Wyler's® or Steero® Chicken-Flavor Instant Bouillon *or* 2 Chicken-Flavor Bouillon Cubes; cook and stir until thickened and bouillon is dissolved. Refrigerate leftovers. (Makes about 1½ cups)

Apple & Herb Stuffing, Rich Turkey Gravy

HERB MARINATED CHICKEN WITH PEACH SALSA

Makes 6 servings

1/2 cup vegetable oil
1/4 cup ReaLemon® Lemon Juice
   from Concentrate
2 cloves garlic, finely chopped
1 tablespoon Wyler's® or Steero®
   Chicken-Flavor Instant
   Bouillon
1 1/2 teaspoons thyme leaves
3 pounds chicken pieces

In large shallow dish or plastic bag, combine all ingredients except chicken; mix well. Add chicken; cover. Marinate in refrigerator 6 hours or overnight, turning chicken occasionally. Remove chicken from marinade; heat marinade thoroughly. Grill or broil chicken about 45 minutes or until cooked, turning and brushing frequently with marinade. Serve with Peach Salsa if desired. Refrigerate leftovers.

PEACH SALSA

2 medium peaches, pitted and
   diced (about 2 cups)
1/2 cup diced red bell pepper
2 tablespoons sliced green onion
2 tablespoons ReaLemon® Lemon
   Juice from Concentrate
2 teaspoons chopped fresh mint
   leaves *or* 1 teaspoon dried
   mint leaves
2 teaspoons vegetable oil
3/4 teaspoon chopped fresh ginger
   root *or* 1/4 teaspoon ground
   ginger
1/2 teaspoon finely chopped,
   seeded jalapeño pepper

In medium bowl, combine ingredients. Cover; chill several hours or overnight. (Makes about 2 cups)

Herb Marinated Chicken with Peach Salsa

TURKEY ROLLS DI NAPOLI

Makes 4 to 6 servings

1 green bell pepper, cut into thin strips
1 red bell pepper, cut into thin strips
1 clove garlic, finely chopped
3 tablespoons olive oil
6 (4-ounce) fresh turkey breast slices, pounded and lightly seasoned with salt and pepper
3 ounces Swiss cheese, cut into 12 strips
1 (26-ounce) jar Classico® Di Napoli (Tomato & Basil) Pasta Sauce
½ (1-pound) package Creamette® Linguine or Rotini, cooked as package directs and drained

In large skillet, cook peppers and garlic in *2 tablespoons* oil until tender; remove from pan. On each turkey slice, place a green and red pepper strip and 2 cheese strips. Roll tightly and secure with wooden picks. In same skillet, heat remaining *1 tablespoon* oil. Over medium-high heat, brown turkey rolls. Add pasta sauce and remaining peppers. Reduce heat; cover and simmer 10 minutes or until hot. Remove picks; serve over hot cooked pasta. Refrigerate leftovers.

Mediterranean Marinated Chicken

MEDITERRANEAN MARINADE

Makes about 1 cup

⅓ cup olive or vegetable oil
¼ cup ReaLemon® Lemon Juice from Concentrate
3 tablespoons dry sherry or water
2 teaspoons rosemary leaves, crushed
2 cloves garlic, finely chopped
1½ teaspoons Wyler's® or Steero® Chicken-Flavor Instant Bouillon

Combine ingredients; mix well. In large shallow dish or plastic bag, pour over chicken, pork or beef. Cover; marinate in refrigerator 4 hours or overnight, turning occasionally. Remove meat from marinade; heat marinade thoroughly. Grill or broil meat as desired, basting frequently with marinade. Refrigerate leftovers.

Turkey Parmesan

TURKEY PARMESAN

Makes 1 serving; 198 calories

1 teaspoon diet margarine
1 (2-ounce) fresh turkey breast
    slice
3 tablespoons Classico® Pasta
    Sauce, any flavor
1 teaspoon grated Parmesan
    cheese
1 slice Borden® Lite-line®
    Process Cheese Product*,
    any flavor

In small skillet, over medium heat,
melt margarine. Add turkey breast
slice. Cook 2 minutes; turn. Reduce
heat to low; top turkey with
remaining ingredients. Cover; cook 2
to 3 minutes longer or until turkey is
no longer pink. Garnish as desired.
Refrigerate leftovers.

*"½ the calories" — 8% milkfat
product
Caloric values by product analyses
and recipe calculation*

CREAMY CHICKEN PICCATA

Makes 6 servings

⅓ cup plus 1 tablespoon unsifted
    flour
½ teaspoon paprika
6 skinned chicken breast halves
    (about 2 pounds)
3 tablespoons margarine or
    butter
2 cups (1 pint) Borden® or
    Meadow Gold® Coffee
    Cream *or* Half-and-Half
¼ cup water
1 tablespoon Wyler's® or Steero®
    Chicken-Flavor Instant
    Bouillon *or* 3 Chicken-Flavor
    Bouillon Cubes
2 tablespoons ReaLemon® Lemon
    Juice from Concentrate
2 tablespoons dry sherry
½ cup (2 ounces) shredded Swiss
    cheese
    Hot cooked rice
    Chopped parsley

In plastic bag, combine *⅓ cup* flour
and paprika. Add chicken, a few
pieces at a time; shake to coat. In
large skillet, over medium heat,
brown chicken in margarine; remove
from pan. Stir in remaining
1 tablespoon flour until smooth.
Gradually add cream, water and
bouillon; over low heat, cook and
stir 5 minutes or until bouillon is
dissolved. Stir in ReaLemon® brand
and sherry; add chicken. Cover;
simmer 20 minutes or until chicken
is tender. Top with cheese. Serve
with rice; garnish with parsley.
Refrigerate leftovers.

Chicken Dijon

CHICKEN DIJON

Makes 4 servings

- ¹/₃ cup plus 1 tablespoon unsifted flour
- ¹/₄ teaspoon paprika
- 2 cups (1 pint) Borden® or Meadow Gold® Half-and-Half
- 2 tablespoons Dijon-style mustard
- ³/₄ teaspoon rosemary leaves
- ³/₄ teaspoon thyme leaves
- 2 teaspoons Wyler's® or Steero® Chicken-Flavor Instant Bouillon
- 4 skinned boneless chicken breast halves (about 1 pound)
- ¹/₄ cup vegetable oil
- 1 cup sliced fresh mushrooms (about 4 ounces)
- ³/₄ cup diced onion
- ³/₄ cup diced red bell pepper Creamette® or Pennsylvania Dutch® Brand Egg Noodles, cooked as package directs and drained

Combine ¹/₃ cup flour and paprika. In medium bowl, combine half-and-half and seasonings; dip chicken in half-and-half mixture then flour. In large skillet, cook chicken in oil until tender. Remove from pan; keep warm. In drippings, cook mushrooms and onion until tender; stir in remaining *1 tablespoon* flour until blended. Add half-and-half mixture. Cook and stir until thickened; simmer 10 minutes. Add red pepper; cook 5 minutes. Serve sauce with chicken and hot cooked noodles. Refrigerate leftovers.

FISH & SEAFOOD

CITRUS MARINATED FISH STEAKS

Makes 4 servings

1/4 cup frozen orange juice concentrate, thawed
1/4 cup ReaLemon® Lemon Juice from Concentrate
1 tablespoon vegetable oil
1/2 teaspoon dill weed
4 (1-inch thick) salmon, halibut or swordfish steaks, fresh or frozen, thawed (about 1 1/2 pounds)

In large shallow dish or plastic bag, combine juices, oil and dill; mix well. Add fish. Cover; marinate in refrigerator 2 hours, turning occasionally. Remove fish from marinade; heat marinade thoroughly. Grill or broil until fish flakes with fork, basting frequently with marinade. Garnish as desired. Refrigerate leftovers.

WHITE CLAM SAUCE

Makes about 2 1/2 cups

2 cloves garlic, finely chopped
1/4 cup olive oil
2 (6 1/2-ounce) cans Doxsee® or Snow's® Minced *or* Chopped Clams, drained, reserving liquid
1 (8-ounce) bottle Doxsee® or Snow's® Clam Juice
1 tablespoon chopped parsley
1/4 teaspoon basil leaves
Dash pepper

In medium saucepan, cook garlic in oil until tender. Add reserved clam liquid, clam juice and seasonings. Bring to a boil. Reduce heat; simmer 5 minutes. Add clams; heat through. Serve over hot cooked Creamette® Linguine topped with grated Parmesan cheese. Refrigerate leftovers.

SEAFOOD KABOBS

Makes 4 servings

1/3 cup pineapple juice
1/3 cup ReaLemon® Lemon Juice from Concentrate *or* ReaLime® Lime Juice from Concentrate
2 tablespoons vegetable oil
1 to 2 tablespoons brown sugar
1 teaspoon grated orange rind
1/4 teaspoon ground cinnamon
3/4 pound large raw shrimp, peeled and deveined
1/2 pound sea scallops
1 cup melon chunks or balls
1 medium avocado, peeled, seeded and cut into chunks

In large shallow dish or plastic bag, combine juices, oil, sugar, rind and cinnamon; mix well. Add seafood and melon. Cover; marinate in refrigerator 4 hours or overnight. Remove seafood and melon from marinade; heat marinade thoroughly. Alternately thread shrimp, scallops, melon and avocado on skewers. Grill or broil 3 to 6 minutes or until shrimp are pink and scallops are opaque, basting frequently with marinade. Refrigerate leftovers.

Top to bottom: Citrus Marinated Fish Steaks and Seafood Kabobs

CRISPY OVEN FISH

Makes 4 servings

2 1/2 cups finely crushed
    Kruncher's!® Potato Chips
1/2 cup grated Parmesan cheese
2 tablespoons chopped parsley
1/2 cup mayonnaise or salad
    dressing
4 tablespoons ReaLemon® Lemon
    Juice from Concentrate
1 pound fish fillets, fresh or
    frozen, thawed

Preheat oven to 400°. Combine chips, cheese and parsley. In small bowl, combine mayonnaise and *2 tablespoons* ReaLemon® brand. Dip fish in remaining *2 tablespoons* ReaLemon® brand, then mayonnaise mixture, then chip mixture. Arrange in greased baking dish. Bake 5 to 10 minutes or until fish flakes with fork. Garnish as desired. Refrigerate leftovers.

Crispy Oven Fish

CALIFORNIA SALMON PIE

Makes one 9-inch pie

1 (9-inch) unbaked pastry shell
4 eggs
1 (15 1/2-ounce) can salmon,
    drained, deboned and flaked
1 (9-ounce) package frozen
    artichoke hearts, cooked,
    drained and chopped *or*
    1 (14-ounce) can artichoke
    hearts, drained and chopped
1/4 cup chopped green onions
1/4 cup grated Parmesan cheese
2 tablespoons margarine or
    butter, melted
3 tablespoons ReaLemon® Lemon
    Juice from Concentrate *or*
    ReaLime® Lime Juice from
    Concentrate
1 1/2 teaspoons Wyler's® or Steero®
    Chicken-Flavor Instant
    Bouillon
1 (8-ounce) container Borden®
    or Meadow Gold® Sour
    Cream, at room temperature
1 1/2 teaspoons dill weed

Preheat oven to 425°. In large bowl, beat eggs; add salmon, artichokes, green onions, cheese, margarine, *1 tablespoon* ReaLemon® brand and *1 teaspoon* bouillon. Pour into pastry shell. Bake 25 minutes. In small bowl, combine sour cream, remaining *2 tablespoons* ReaLemon® brand, remaining *1/2 teaspoon* bouillon and dill. Spread over salmon filling; bake 5 minutes longer or until set. Serve warm or chilled. Garnish as desired. Refrigerate leftovers.

Sweet and Sour Shrimp

SWEET AND SOUR SHRIMP

Makes 4 servings

- 1 (20-ounce) can juice-pack pineapple chunks, drained, reserving juice
- ³/₄ cup cold water
- ¹/₃ cup ReaLemon® Lemon Juice from Concentrate
- ¹/₃ cup firmly packed light brown sugar
- 3 tablespoons cornstarch
- 3 tablespoons soy sauce
- ¹/₈ teaspoon ground ginger
- 1 pound medium raw shrimp, peeled and deveined
- 1 (8-ounce) can sliced water chestnuts, drained
- 1 green bell pepper, cut into chunks
  Hot cooked rice

In large skillet, combine reserved pineapple juice, water, ReaLemon® brand, sugar, cornstarch, soy sauce and ginger. Over medium heat, cook and stir until thickened. Add shrimp; cook until pink, about 3 minutes. Add remaining ingredients except rice; heat through. Serve with rice. Refrigerate leftovers.

ALMONDINE FISH

Makes 4 servings

- ¹/₂ cup margarine or butter, melted
- 3 tablespoons ReaLemon® Lemon Juice from Concentrate
- 3 tablespoons sliced almonds, toasted
- 1 pound fish fillets, fresh or frozen, thawed

Combine margarine and ReaLemon® brand; reserve ¹/₄ cup for basting. Add almonds to remaining margarine mixture; set aside. Broil or grill fish as desired, basting frequently with reserved margarine mixture. Serve with almond sauce. Refrigerate leftovers.

HERB FISH: Omit almonds. Add 1 teaspoon dill weed.

GARLIC FISH: Omit almonds. Add ¹/₂ teaspoon garlic powder.

Fish Rolls Primavera

FISH ROLLS PRIMAVERA

Makes 4 servings

1 cup shredded carrots
1 cup shredded zucchini
2 tablespoons finely chopped onion
1/2 cup fresh bread crumbs (1 slice)
1/8 teaspoon thyme leaves
1/4 cup margarine or butter, melted
1/4 cup ReaLemon® Lemon Juice from Concentrate
4 fish fillets, fresh or frozen, thawed (about 1 pound)

Preheat oven to 375°. In medium bowl, combine vegetables, crumbs and thyme. Combine margarine and ReaLemon® brand; add 1/4 cup to vegetable mixture. Place fillets in shallow baking dish; top with equal amounts of vegetable mixture. Roll up. Pour remaining margarine mixture over fillets. Bake 15 minutes or until fish flakes with fork. Garnish as desired. Refrigerate leftovers.

HOT CRAB MELT

Makes 4 servings

1 (6-ounce) can Harris® or Orleans® Crab Meat, drained
1/4 cup Bennett's® Cocktail *or* Tartar Sauce
2 tablespoons finely chopped celery
2 tablespoons finely chopped green bell pepper
2 English muffins, split and toasted
4 slices Borden® Process American Cheese Food

Preheat oven to 350°. In small bowl, combine crab meat, sauce, celery and green pepper; spread equal amounts on muffin halves. Bake 5 minutes. Top each with cheese food slice; bake 5 minutes longer or until melted. Serve immediately. Refrigerate leftovers.

SCALLOPS PRIMAVERA

Makes 4 servings

1 pound scallops
¼ cup ReaLemon® Lemon Juice from Concentrate
1 cup thinly sliced carrots
3 cloves garlic, finely chopped
⅓ cup margarine or butter
8 ounces fresh mushrooms, sliced (about 2 cups)
¾ teaspoon thyme leaves
2 teaspoons cornstarch
½ teaspoon salt
¼ cup diagonally sliced green onions
4 ounces fresh pea pods *or* 1 (6-ounce) package frozen pea pods, thawed
2 tablespoons dry sherry
Hot cooked rice

In large shallow dish or plastic bag, combine scallops and ReaLemon® brand. Cover; marinate in refrigerator 30 to 60 minutes, stirring occasionally. In large skillet, over high heat, cook and stir carrots and garlic in margarine until tender-crisp, about 3 minutes. Add mushrooms and thyme; cook and stir about 5 minutes. Stir cornstarch and salt into scallop mixture; add to skillet. Cook and stir until scallops are opaque, about 4 minutes. Add green onions, pea pods and sherry; heat through. Serve with rice. Refrigerate leftovers.

Scallops Primavera

Scampi-Style Shrimp

SCAMPI-STYLE SHRIMP

Makes 4 servings

2 tablespoons sliced green onion
4 cloves garlic, finely chopped
2 tablespoons margarine or butter
2 tablespoons olive or vegetable oil
1 pound medium raw shrimp, peeled and deveined
¼ cup ReaLemon® Lemon Juice from Concentrate
⅛ teaspoon salt
Chopped parsley

In large skillet, over medium-high heat, cook and stir green onion and garlic in margarine and oil 1 minute. Add shrimp; cook and stir until shrimp are pink, about 3 minutes. Add ReaLemon® brand and salt; heat through. Garnish with parsley. Refrigerate leftovers.

Desserts

PIES

REALEMON MERINGUE PIE

Makes one 9-inch pie

1 (9-inch) baked pastry shell
1²/₃ cups sugar
6 tablespoons cornstarch
½ cup ReaLemon® Lemon Juice
   from Concentrate
4 eggs, separated
1½ cups boiling water
2 tablespoons margarine or
   butter
¼ teaspoon cream of tartar

Preheat oven to 300°. In heavy medium saucepan, combine 1¹/₃ cups sugar and cornstarch; add ReaLemon® brand. In small bowl, beat egg *yolks*; add to lemon mixture. Gradually add water, stirring constantly. Over medium heat, cook and stir until mixture boils and thickens, about 8 to 10 minutes. Remove from heat. Add margarine; stir until melted. Pour into prepared pastry shell. In small mixer bowl, beat egg *whites* with cream of tartar until soft peaks form; gradually add remaining ¹/₃ cup sugar, beating until stiff but not dry. Spread on top of pie, sealing carefully to edge of shell. Bake 20 to 30 minutes or until golden. Cool. Chill before serving. Refrigerate leftovers.

FUDGE BROWNIE PIE

Makes one 9-inch pie

1 (9-inch) unbaked pastry shell
1 cup (6 ounces) semi-sweet
   chocolate chips
¼ cup margarine or butter
1 (14-ounce) can Eagle® Brand
   Sweetened Condensed Milk
   (NOT evaporated milk)
½ cup biscuit baking mix
2 eggs
1 teaspoon vanilla extract
1 cup chopped nuts

Preheat oven to 375°. Bake pastry shell 10 minutes; remove from oven. *Reduce oven temperature to 325°.* In small saucepan, over low heat, melt chips with margarine. In large mixer bowl, beat chocolate mixture with sweetened condensed milk, biscuit mix, eggs and vanilla until smooth. Add nuts. Pour into prepared pastry shell. Bake 35 to 45 minutes or until center is set. Cool. Serve warm or at room temperature with ice cream if desired.

ReaLemon Meringue Pie

Sour Cream Mince Pie

SOUR CREAM MINCE PIE

Makes one 9-inch pie

1 (9-inch) unbaked pastry shell
1 (9-ounce) package None Such®
  Condensed Mincemeat,
  crumbled
1 cup apple juice or water
1 tablespoon flour
1 medium all-purpose apple,
  cored, pared and chopped
1 (16-ounce) container Borden®
  or Meadow Gold® Sour
  Cream
2 eggs
2 tablespoons sugar
1 teaspoon vanilla extract
2 to 3 tablespoons chopped nuts

Preheat oven to 425°. In small
saucepan, combine mincemeat and
apple juice. Bring to a boil; boil
briskly 1 minute. In medium bowl,
stir flour into apple to coat; stir in
mincemeat. Pour into pastry shell.
Bake 25 minutes. Meanwhile, in
small mixer bowl, combine sour
cream, eggs, sugar and vanilla; beat
until smooth. Pour evenly over
baked filling. Sprinkle with nuts.
Reduce oven temperature to 325°;
bake 20 minutes longer or until set.
Cool. Chill thoroughly. Garnish as
desired. Refrigerate leftovers.

KEY LIME PIE

Makes one 9- or 10-inch pie

1 (9- or 10-inch) baked pastry
  shell or graham cracker
  crumb crust*
6 egg *yolks*
2 (14-ounce) cans Eagle® Brand
  Sweetened Condensed Milk
  (NOT evaporated milk)
1 (8-ounce) bottle ReaLime®
  Lime Juice from Concentrate
  Yellow or green food coloring,
  optional
  Borden® or Meadow Gold®
  Whipping Cream, whipped
  or whipped topping

Preheat oven to 325°. In large mixer
bowl, beat egg *yolks*; stir in
sweetened condensed milk,
ReaLime® brand and food coloring if
desired. Pour into prepared pastry
shell; bake 40 minutes. Cool. Chill.
Spread top with whipped cream.
Garnish as desired. Refrigerate
leftovers.

*If using frozen packaged pie shell
or 6-ounce packaged graham cracker
crumb crust, use 1 can Eagle® Brand
Sweetened Condensed Milk, 3 egg
yolks and 1/2 cup ReaLime® brand.
Bake 30 minutes. Proceed as above.*

Key Lime Pie

Strawberry Cheese Pie

STRAWBERRY CHEESE PIE

Makes one 9-inch pie

1 (9-inch) baked pastry shell or
   graham cracker crumb crust
1 (8-ounce) package cream
   cheese, softened
1 (14-ounce) can Eagle® Brand
   Sweetened Condensed Milk
   (NOT evaporated milk)
1/3 cup ReaLemon® Lemon Juice
   from Concentrate
1 teaspoon vanilla extract
1 quart (about 1½ pounds) fresh
   strawberries, cleaned and
   hulled
1 (16-ounce) package prepared
   strawberry glaze, chilled

In large mixer bowl, beat cheese
until fluffy. Gradually beat in
sweetened condensed milk until
smooth. Stir in ReaLemon® brand
and vanilla. Pour into prepared
pastry shell. Chill 3 hours or until
set. Top with strawberries and
desired amount of glaze. Refrigerate
leftovers.

CHERRY CHEESE PIE: Omit
strawberries and glaze. Top with
1 (21-ounce) can cherry pie filling,
chilled.

MICROWAVE CHOCOLATE MOUSSE PIE

Makes one 9-inch pie

- 1 (9-inch) baked pastry shell
- 4 (1-ounce) squares unsweetened chocolate
- 1 (14-ounce) can Eagle® Brand Sweetened Condensed Milk (NOT evaporated milk)
- 2 teaspoons vanilla extract
- 2 cups (1 pint) Borden® or Meadow Gold® Whipping Cream, whipped

In 2-quart glass measure with handle, combine chocolate, sweetened condensed milk and vanilla; cook on 100% power (high) 2 to 4 minutes, stirring after each minute until chocolate is melted and mixture is smooth. Cool to room temperature, about 1½ hours. Beat until smooth. Fold in whipped cream. Pour into prepared pastry shell. Chill 4 hours or until set. Garnish as desired. Refrigerate leftovers.

Microwave Chocolate Mousse Pie

CLASSIC PEANUT BUTTER PIE

Makes one 9-inch pie

- 1 (9-inch) baked pastry shell
- ½ cup peanut butter
- ¾ cup confectioners' sugar
- ¼ cup chopped peanuts
- 1 (14-ounce) can Eagle® Brand Sweetened Condensed Milk (NOT evaporated milk)
- 4 egg *yolks*
- ½ cup water
- 1 (4-serving size) package vanilla flavor pudding mix (*not instant*)
- 1 (8-ounce) container Borden® or Meadow Gold® Sour Cream, at room temperature Borden® or Meadow Gold® Whipping Cream, whipped *or* whipped topping

In small bowl, cut peanut butter into confectioners' sugar until crumbly; stir in peanuts. Sprinkle into prepared pastry shell. In medium saucepan, combine sweetened condensed milk, egg *yolks*, water and pudding mix. Over medium heat, cook and stir until thickened. Cool 15 minutes; beat in sour cream. Spoon into prepared pastry shell. Chill thoroughly. Spread top with whipped cream. Garnish as desired. Refrigerate leftovers.

MICROWAVE: Prepare crumb mixture as above. In 2-quart glass measure with handle, combine sweetened condensed milk, egg *yolks*, water and pudding mix; mix well. Cook on 100% power (high) 5 to 8 minutes, stirring after 2 minutes then every minute until thickened and smooth. Proceed as above.

Fresh Apple Custard Pie

FRESH APPLE CUSTARD PIE

Makes one 9-inch pie

1 (9-inch) unbaked pastry shell
1½ cups Borden® or Meadow
    Gold® Sour Cream
1 (14-ounce) can Eagle® Brand
    Sweetened Condensed Milk
    (NOT evaporated milk)
¼ cup frozen apple juice
    concentrate, thawed
1 egg
1½ teaspoons vanilla extract
¼ teaspoon ground cinnamon
3 medium all-purpose apples,
    cored, pared and thinly
    sliced
2 tablespoons margarine or
    butter
Apple Cinnamon Glaze

Preheat oven to 375°. Bake pastry shell 15 minutes. Meanwhile, in small mixer bowl, beat sour cream, sweetened condensed milk, juice concentrate, egg, vanilla and cinnamon until smooth. Pour into prepared pastry shell; bake 30 minutes or until set. Cool. In large skillet, cook apples in margarine until tender-crisp. Arrange on top of pie; drizzle with Apple Cinnamon Glaze. Serve warm or chilled. Refrigerate leftovers.

Apple Cinnamon Glaze

In small saucepan, combine ¼ cup thawed frozen apple juice concentrate, 1 teaspoon cornstarch and ¼ teaspoon ground cinnamon; mix well. Over low heat, cook and stir until thickened. (Makes about ¼ cup)

Fluffy Grasshopper Pie

FLUFFY GRASSHOPPER PIE

Makes one 9-inch pie

- **2 cups finely crushed creme-filled chocolate sandwich cookies (about 24 cookies)**
- **1/4 cup margarine or butter, melted**
- **1 (8-ounce) package cream cheese, softened**
- **1 (14-ounce) can Eagle® Brand Sweetened Condensed Milk (NOT evaporated milk)**
- **3 tablespoons ReaLemon® Lemon Juice from Concentrate**
- **1/4 cup green crème de menthe liqueur**
- **1/4 cup white crème de cacao liqueur**
- **1 (4-ounce) container frozen non-dairy whipped topping, thawed (1 3/4 cups)**

Combine crumbs and margarine; press firmly on bottom and up side to rim of buttered 9-inch pie plate to form crust. Chill. Meanwhile, in large mixer bowl, beat cheese until fluffy. Gradually beat in sweetened condensed milk until smooth. Stir in ReaLemon® brand and liqueurs. Fold in whipped topping. Chill 20 minutes; pour into prepared crust. Chill or freeze 4 hours or until set. Garnish as desired. Refrigerate or freeze leftovers.

TRADITIONAL PUMPKIN PIE

Makes one 9-inch pie

- **1 (9-inch) unbaked pastry shell**
- **1 (16-ounce) can pumpkin (about 2 cups)**
- **1 (14-ounce) can Eagle® Brand Sweetened Condensed Milk (NOT evaporated milk)**
- **2 eggs**
- **1 teaspoon ground cinnamon**
- **1/2 teaspoon *each:* ground ginger, nutmeg and salt**

Preheat oven to 425°. In large mixer bowl, combine filling ingredients; mix well. Pour into pastry shell. Bake 15 minutes. *Reduce oven temperature to 350°;* bake 35 minutes longer or until knife inserted near edge comes out clean. Cool. Refrigerate leftovers.

CREAMY LEMON PIE

Makes one 8- or 9-inch pie

- **1 (8- or 9-inch) baked pastry shell or graham cracker crumb crust**
- **3 egg *yolks***
- **1 (14-ounce) can Eagle® Brand Sweetened Condensed Milk (NOT evaporated milk)**
- **1/2 cup ReaLemon® Lemon Juice from Concentrate**
  Yellow food coloring, optional
  Borden® or Meadow Gold® Whipping Cream, whipped

Preheat oven to 325°. In medium bowl, beat egg *yolks;* stir in sweetened condensed milk, ReaLemon® brand and food coloring if desired. Pour into prepared pastry shell; bake 30 minutes. Cool. Chill. Spread top with whipped cream. Refrigerate leftovers.

FROZEN STRAWBERRY MARGARITA PIE

Makes one 9-inch pie

1¼ cups *finely* crushed Seyfert's® or Quinlan® Pretzels

½ cup plus 2 tablespoons margarine or butter, melted

¼ cup sugar

1 (14-ounce) can Eagle® Brand Sweetened Condensed Milk (NOT evaporated milk)

1½ cups chopped fresh or frozen unsweetened strawberries, thawed and *well drained*

⅓ cup ReaLime® Lime Juice from Concentrate

2 tablespoons tequila

2 tablespoons triple sec or other orange-flavored liqueur

Red food coloring, optional

1½ cups Borden® or Meadow Gold® Whipping Cream, whipped

Combine crushed pretzels, margarine and sugar; press firmly on bottom and up side to rim of lightly buttered 9-inch pie plate to form crust. In large bowl, combine sweetened condensed milk, chopped strawberries, ReaLime® brand, tequila, triple sec and food coloring if desired; mix well. Fold in whipped cream. Pour into prepared crust. Freeze 4 hours or until firm. Let stand 10 minutes before serving. Garnish as desired. Freeze ungarnished leftovers.

FROZEN MARGARITA PIE: Omit strawberries and red food coloring. Proceed as above.

Left to right: Frozen Strawberry Margarita Pie and Frozen Margarita Pie

Left to right: Frozen Peach Melba Pie and Lime Parfait Ice Cream Pie

FROZEN PEACH MELBA PIE

Makes one 9-inch pie

**2 cups *crushed* granola or
  natural cereal**
3 tablespoons flour
**3 tablespoons margarine or
  butter, melted**
2 teaspoons ground cinnamon
**1 (10-ounce) package frozen red
  raspberries in syrup, thawed
  and drained, reserving
  ²/₃ cup syrup**
¼ cup Bama® Red Currant Jelly
1 tablespoon cornstarch
¼ teaspoon almond extract
**½ (½-gallon) carton Borden® or
  Meadow Gold® Peach
  Premium Frozen Yogurt,
  slightly softened**

Preheat oven to 375°. In medium bowl, combine granola, flour, margarine and cinnamon; press on bottom and up side to rim of 9-inch pie plate to form crust. Bake 8 to 10 minutes. Cool. In small saucepan, combine reserved raspberry syrup, jelly and cornstarch. Over medium heat, cook and stir until slightly thickened and glossy; stir in extract and raspberries. Cool. Scoop yogurt into prepared crust; top with raspberry sauce. Freeze 6 hours or until firm. Remove from freezer 5 to 10 minutes before serving. Garnish as desired. Freeze ungarnished leftovers.

LIME PARFAIT ICE CREAM PIE

Makes one 9-inch pie

Coconut Crust or 1 (9-inch) baked pastry shell
½ cup butter or margarine
1 cup sugar
½ cup ReaLime® Lime Juice from Concentrate
¼ teaspoon salt
3 egg *yolks*
2 eggs
Green food coloring, optional
1½ quarts Borden® or Meadow Gold® Vanilla Ice Cream, slightly softened

Prepare crust. In medium saucepan, melt butter; add sugar, ReaLime® brand and salt. Mix well. In small bowl, beat egg *yolks* and eggs; gradually add to lime mixture. Over low heat, cook and stir constantly until smooth and thick; add food coloring if desired. Cool. Spoon half the sauce into prepared crust. Scoop ice cream into prepared crust; top with remaining sauce and reserved coconut mixture from crust. Freeze 6 hours or until firm. Remove from freezer 10 minutes before serving. Freeze leftovers.

Coconut Crust

Toast 1 (7-ounce) package flaked coconut (2⅔ cups); combine with ⅓ cup butter or margarine, melted. Reserving 2 tablespoons, press remainder firmly on bottom and up side to rim of 9-inch pie plate. Chill. (Makes one 9-inch crust)

TIP: To toast coconut, spread evenly in shallow pan. Toast in preheated 350° oven 7 to 15 minutes or until golden, stirring frequently.

MAPLE PECAN PIE

Makes one 9-inch pie

1 (9-inch) unbaked pastry shell
3 eggs, beaten
1 cup Cary's®, MacDonald's™ or Maple Orchards® Pure Maple Syrup
½ cup firmly packed light brown sugar
2 tablespoons margarine or butter, melted
1 teaspoon vanilla extract
1¼ cups pecan halves or pieces

Place rack in lowest position in oven; preheat oven to 350°. In large bowl, combine all ingredients except pastry shell. Pour into pastry shell. Bake 35 to 40 minutes or until golden. Cool. Serve at room temperature or chilled. Refrigerate leftovers.

Maple Pecan Pie

CAKES & COOKIES

STRAWBERRY BROWNIE TORTE

Makes 10 to 12 servings

- 1 (21.5- or 23.6-ounce) package fudge brownie mix
- 1 (14-ounce) can Eagle® Brand Sweetened Condensed Milk (NOT evaporated milk)
- 1/2 cup cold water
- 1 (4-serving size) package *instant* vanilla flavor pudding mix
- 1 (4-ounce) container frozen non-dairy whipped topping, thawed (1 3/4 cups)
- 1 quart (about 1 1/2 pounds) fresh strawberries, cleaned, hulled and halved

Preheat oven to 350°. Grease two 9-inch round layer cake pans. Line with wax paper, extending up sides of pans; grease wax paper. Prepare brownie mix as package directs for cake-like brownies; pour into prepared pans. Bake 20 minutes or until tops spring back when touched. Remove from pans; cool. In large bowl, mix sweetened condensed milk and water; beat in pudding mix. Chill 5 minutes. Fold in whipped topping. Place 1 brownie layer on serving plate. Top with half *each* the pudding mixture and strawberries. Repeat layers. Drizzle with chocolate-flavored syrup if desired. Refrigerate leftovers.

MICROWAVE CHEESECAKE

Makes one 10-inch cheesecake

- 1/3 cup margarine or butter
- 1 1/4 cups graham cracker crumbs
- 1/4 cup sugar
- 2 (8-ounce) packages cream cheese, softened
- 1 (14-ounce) can Eagle® Brand Sweetened Condensed Milk (NOT evaporated milk)
- 3 eggs
- 1/4 cup ReaLemon® Lemon Juice from Concentrate
- 1 (8-ounce) container Borden® or Meadow Gold® Sour Cream, at room temperature

In 10-inch microwave-safe quiche dish or pie plate, melt margarine loosely covered on 100% power (high) 1 minute. Add crumbs and sugar; press firmly on bottom of dish. Cook on 100% power (high) 1 1/2 minutes, rotating dish once. In 2-quart glass measure with handle, beat cheese until fluffy. Gradually beat in sweetened condensed milk until smooth. Add eggs then ReaLemon® brand; mix well. Cook on 70% power (medium-high) 6 to 8 minutes or until hot, stirring every 2 minutes. Pour into prepared crust. Cook on 50% power (medium) 6 to 8 minutes or until center is set, rotating dish once. Top with sour cream. Cool. Chill. Serve with fruit if desired. Refrigerate leftovers.

Strawberry Brownie Torte

Left to right: Magic Cookie Bars and Choco-Dipped Peanut Butter Cookies

EASY PEANUT BUTTER COOKIES

Makes about 5 dozen cookies

1 (14-ounce) can Eagle® Brand
    Sweetened Condensed Milk
    (NOT evaporated milk)
3/4 to 1 cup peanut butter
1 egg
1 teaspoon vanilla extract
2 cups biscuit baking mix
    Granulated sugar

Preheat oven to 350°. In large mixer bowl, beat sweetened condensed milk, peanut butter, egg and vanilla until smooth. Add biscuit mix; mix well. Cover; chill at least 1 hour. Shape into 1-inch balls. Roll in sugar. Place 2 inches apart on ungreased baking sheets. Flatten with fork. Bake 6 to 8 minutes or until lightly browned (*do not overbake*). Cool. Store tightly covered at room temperature.

CHOCO-DIPPED PEANUT BUTTER COOKIES: Shape as directed; omit granulated sugar. *Do not flatten.* Bake as above. Cool. Melt 1 pound Eagle™ Brand Chocolate-Flavored Candy Coating. Partially dip each cookie into candy coating. Place on wax paper-lined baking sheets. Let stand or chill until firm.

PEANUT BLOSSOMS: Shape as directed; *do not flatten*. Bake as above. Press solid milk chocolate candy drop in center of each cookie immediately after baking.

MAGIC COOKIE BARS

Makes 24 to 36 bars

¹/₂ cup margarine or butter
1¹/₂ cups graham cracker crumbs
1 (14-ounce) can Eagle® Brand Sweetened Condensed Milk (NOT evaporated milk)
1 cup (6 ounces) semi-sweet chocolate chips
1 (3¹/₂-ounce) can flaked coconut (1¹/₃ cups)
1 cup chopped walnuts

Preheat oven to 350° (325° for glass dish). In 13×9-inch baking pan, melt margarine in oven. Sprinkle crumbs over margarine; pour sweetened condensed milk evenly over crumbs. Top with remaining ingredients; press down firmly. Bake 25 to 30 minutes or until lightly browned. Cool. Chill if desired. Cut into bars. Store loosely covered at room temperature.

SEVEN LAYER MAGIC COOKIE BARS: Add 1 (6-ounce) package butterscotch flavored chips after chocolate chips.

MINI CHEESECAKES

Makes about 2 dozen

1¹/₂ cups graham cracker or chocolate wafer crumbs
¹/₄ cup sugar
¹/₄ cup margarine or butter, melted
3 (8-ounce) packages cream cheese, softened
1 (14-ounce) can Eagle® Brand Sweetened Condensed Milk (NOT evaporated milk)
3 eggs
2 teaspoons vanilla extract

Preheat oven to 300°. Combine crumbs, sugar and margarine; press equal portions on bottoms of 24 lightly greased* or paper-lined muffin cups. In large mixer bowl, beat cheese until fluffy. Gradually beat in sweetened condensed milk until smooth. Add eggs and vanilla; mix well. Spoon equal amounts of mixture (about 3 tablespoons) into prepared cups. Bake 20 minutes or until tops spring back when lightly touched. Cool. Chill. Garnish as desired. Refrigerate leftovers.

CHOCOLATE MINI CHEESECAKES: Melt 1 cup (6 ounces) semi-sweet chocolate chips; mix into batter. Proceed as above. Bake 20 to 25 minutes.

If greased muffin cups are used, cool baked cheesecakes. Freeze 15 minutes; remove with narrow spatula. Proceed as above.

Mini Cheesecakes

Caramel Fudge Cake

CARAMEL FUDGE CAKE

Makes one 13×9-inch cake

1 (18¼- or 18½-ounce) package
    chocolate cake mix
1 (14-ounce) package Eagle™
    Brand Caramels, unwrapped
½ cup margarine or butter
1 (14-ounce) can Eagle® Brand
    Sweetened Condensed Milk
    (NOT evaporated milk)
1 cup coarsely chopped pecans

Preheat oven to 350°. Prepare cake
mix as package directs. Pour *2 cups*
batter into greased 13×9-inch baking
pan; bake 15 minutes. Meanwhile,
in heavy saucepan, over low heat,
melt caramels and margarine with
sweetened condensed milk, stirring
until smooth. Spread evenly over
cake; spread remaining cake batter
over caramel mixture. Top with nuts.
Return to oven; bake 30 to 35
minutes longer or until cake springs
back when lightly touched. Cool.
Garnish as desired.

RICH LEMON BARS

Makes 24 to 36 bars

1½ cups plus 3 tablespoons
    unsifted flour
½ cup confectioners' sugar
¾ cup *cold* margarine or butter
4 eggs, slightly beaten
1½ cups granulated sugar
1 teaspoon baking powder
½ cup ReaLemon® Lemon Juice
    from Concentrate
Additional confectioners' sugar

Preheat oven to 350°. In medium
bowl, combine *1½ cups* flour and
½ cup confectioners' sugar; cut in
margarine until crumbly. Press onto
bottom of lightly greased 13×9-inch
baking pan; bake 15 minutes.
Meanwhile, in large bowl, combine
eggs, granulated sugar, baking
powder, ReaLemon® brand and
remaining *3 tablespoons* flour; mix
well. Pour over baked crust; bake
20 to 25 minutes or until golden
brown. Cool. Cut into bars. Sprinkle
with additional confectioners' sugar.
Store covered in refrigerator; serve at
room temperature.

LEMON PECAN BARS: Omit 3
tablespoons flour in lemon mixture.
Sprinkle ¾ cup finely chopped
pecans over top of lemon mixture.
Bake as above.

LEMON COCONUT BARS: Omit 3
tablespoons flour in lemon mixture.
Sprinkle ¾ cup flaked coconut over
top of lemon mixture. Bake as
above.

Rich Lemon Coconut Bars

Creamy Baked Cheesecake

CREAMY BAKED CHEESECAKE

Makes one 9-inch cheesecake

1¼ cups graham cracker crumbs
¼ cup sugar
⅓ cup margarine or butter, melted
2 (8-ounce) packages cream cheese, softened
1 (14-ounce) can Eagle® Brand Sweetened Condensed Milk (NOT evaporated milk)
3 eggs
¼ cup ReaLemon® Lemon Juice from Concentrate
1 (8-ounce) container Borden® or Meadow Gold® Sour Cream, at room temperature
Fresh strawberries, hulled and sliced

Preheat oven to 300°. Combine crumbs, sugar and margarine; press firmly on bottom of 9-inch springform pan. In large mixer bowl, beat cheese until fluffy. Gradually beat in sweetened condensed milk until smooth. Add eggs and ReaLemon® brand; mix well. Pour into prepared pan. Bake 50 to 55 minutes or until center is set; top with sour cream. Bake 5 minutes longer. Cool. Chill. Just before serving, remove side of springform pan. Top with strawberries. Refrigerate leftovers.

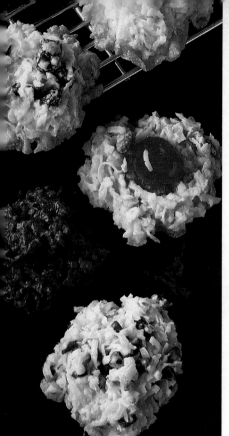

Coconut Macaroons

COCONUT MACAROONS

Makes about 4 dozen cookies

**2 (7-ounce) packages *flaked*
   coconut (5⅓ cups)**
**1 (14-ounce) can Eagle® Brand
   Sweetened Condensed Milk
   (NOT evaporated milk)**
2 teaspoons vanilla extract
1½ teaspoons almond extract

Preheat oven to 350°. In large bowl,
combine coconut, sweetened
condensed milk and extracts; mix
well. Drop by rounded teaspoonfuls
onto aluminum foil-lined and
generously greased baking sheets;
garnish as desired. Bake 8 to 10
minutes or until lightly browned
around edges. *Immediately* remove
from baking sheets (macaroons will
stick if allowed to cool). Store
loosely covered at room
temperature.

VARIATIONS

Macaroon Kisses: Prepare and bake
as directed. Press solid milk
chocolate candy star or drop in
center of each macaroon
immediately after baking.

Chocolate: Omit almond extract.
Add 4 (1-ounce) squares
unsweetened chocolate, melted.
Proceed as directed.

Chocolate Chip: Omit almond
extract. Add 1 cup mini chocolate
chips. Proceed as directed.

Cherry Nut: Omit almond extract.
Add 1 cup chopped nuts and 2
tablespoons maraschino cherry
syrup. Press maraschino cherry half
into center of each macaroon before
baking. Proceed as directed.

Rum Raisin: Omit almond extract.
Add 1 cup raisins and 1 teaspoon
rum flavoring. Proceed as directed.

Almond Brickle: Add ½ cup
almond brickle chips. Proceed as
directed. Bake 10 to 12 minutes.
Cool 3 minutes; remove from baking
sheets.

Maple Walnut: Omit almond extract.
Add ½ cup finely chopped walnuts
and ½ teaspoon maple flavoring.
Proceed as directed.

Nutty Oat: Omit almond extract.
Add 1 cup oats and 1 cup chopped
nuts. Proceed as directed.

TIP: To reduce cost, omit 1 (7-ounce)
package coconut and substitute 2
cups fresh bread crumbs (4 slices).

GOLDEN CARROT CAKE

Makes one 10-inch cake

- 1 (9-ounce) package None Such® Condensed Mincemeat, crumbled
- 2 cups finely shredded carrots
- 1/2 cup chopped nuts
- 2 teaspoons grated orange rind
- 2 cups unsifted flour
- 1 cup firmly packed light brown sugar
- 3/4 cup vegetable oil
- 4 eggs
- 2 teaspoons baking powder
- 1 teaspoon baking soda
- 1 teaspoon salt
  Orange Glaze

Preheat oven to 325°. In large bowl, combine mincemeat, carrots, nuts and rind; toss with 1/2 cup flour. Set aside. In large mixer bowl, combine sugar and oil; beat well. Add eggs, 1 at a time, beating well after each addition. Combine remaining 1 1/2 cups flour, baking powder, baking soda and salt; gradually add to sugar mixture, beating until smooth. Stir in mincemeat mixture. Turn into *well-greased* and floured 10-inch fluted tube or tube pan. Bake 50 to 60 minutes or until wooden pick inserted near center comes out clean. Cool 10 minutes; remove from pan. Cool. Drizzle with Orange Glaze.

Orange Glaze

Melt 2 tablespoons margarine or butter with 4 teaspoons orange juice in small saucepan. Add 1 cup confectioners' sugar and 1 teaspoon grated orange rind; mix well. (Makes about 1/2 cup)

CARROT CAKE BARS: Grease and flour 15×10-inch baking pan; spread batter evenly in pan. Bake 30 to 35 minutes. Cool completely. Glaze. Cut into bars. (Makes 36 to 48 bars)

Left to right: Golden Carrot Cake and Carrot Cake Bars

Left to right: Streusel Caramel Bars and Triple Layer Chocolate Bars

STREUSEL CARAMEL BARS

Makes 24 to 36 bars

2 cups unsifted flour
³/₄ cup firmly packed light brown sugar
1 egg, beaten
³/₄ cup *cold* margarine or butter
³/₄ cup chopped nuts
24 Eagle™ Brand Caramels, unwrapped
1 (14-ounce) can Eagle® Brand Sweetened Condensed Milk (NOT evaporated milk)

Preheat oven to 350°. In large bowl, combine flour, sugar and egg; cut in ¹/₂ *cup* margarine until crumbly. Stir in nuts. Reserving 2 cups crumb mixture, press remainder firmly on bottom of greased 13×9-inch baking pan. Bake 15 minutes. Meanwhile, in heavy saucepan, over low heat, melt caramels with sweetened condensed milk and remaining ¹/₄ *cup* margarine. Pour over prepared crust. Top with reserved crumb mixture. Bake 30 minutes or until bubbly. Cool. Cut into bars. Store loosely covered at room temperature.

CHOCOLATE CARAMEL BARS: Melt 2 (1-ounce) squares unsweetened chocolate with caramels, sweetened condensed milk and margarine. Proceed as above.

TRIPLE LAYER CHOCOLATE BARS

Makes 24 to 36 bars

1½ cups graham cracker crumbs
½ cup unsweetened cocoa
¼ cup sugar
⅓ cup margarine or butter, melted
1 (14-ounce) can Eagle® Brand Sweetened Condensed Milk (NOT evaporated milk)
¼ cup unsifted flour
1 egg
1 teaspoon vanilla extract
½ teaspoon baking powder
¾ cup chopped nuts
2 cups (12 ounces) semi-sweet chocolate chips

Preheat oven to 350°. Combine crumbs, ¼ cup cocoa, sugar and margarine; press firmly on bottom of 13×9-inch baking pan. In large mixer bowl, beat sweetened condensed milk, flour, remaining ¼ cup cocoa, egg, vanilla and baking powder. Stir in nuts. Spread evenly over prepared crust. Top with chips. Bake 20 to 25 minutes or until set. Cool. Cut into bars. Store tightly covered at room temperature.

EASY BISCUIT SHORTCAKE

Makes one 9-inch cake

3 cups biscuit baking mix
3 tablespoons sugar
3 tablespoons butter or margarine, melted
1 cup Borden® or Meadow Gold® Buttermilk
Additional butter or margarine, melted, optional
Sliced fresh peaches or strawberries
Borden® or Meadow Gold® Whipping Cream, whipped

Preheat oven to 425°. In large bowl, combine biscuit mix and sugar. Stir in *3 tablespoons* melted butter and buttermilk; mix well. Spread in greased 9-inch round layer pan or 9-inch square pan. Bake 20 to 25 minutes or until golden. Brush with additional melted butter if desired. Cool 5 minutes; remove from pan. Split into 2 layers. Serve warm or cool with fruit and whipped cream. Refrigerate leftovers.

CHOCOLATE MAPLE NUT BARS

Makes 24 to 36 bars

1½ cups unsifted flour
⅔ cup sugar
½ teaspoon salt
¾ cup *cold* margarine or butter
2 eggs
1 (14-ounce) can Eagle® Brand Sweetened Condensed Milk (NOT evaporated milk)
1½ teaspoons maple flavoring
2 cups chopped nuts
1 cup (6 ounces) semi-sweet chocolate chips

Preheat oven to 350°. In large bowl, combine flour, sugar and salt; cut in margarine until crumbly. Stir in *1 beaten egg*. Press firmly on bottom of 13×9-inch baking pan. Bake 25 minutes. Meanwhile, in medium bowl, beat sweetened condensed milk, remaining *1 egg* and flavoring; stir in nuts. Sprinkle chips evenly over baked crust. Top with nut mixture; bake 25 minutes longer or until golden. Cool. Cut into bars. Store tightly covered at room temperature.

Chocolate Nut Brownies

CHOCOLATE NUT BROWNIES

Makes 24 to 36 brownies

**2 cups (12 ounces) semi-sweet
  chocolate chips**
¼ cup margarine or butter
2 cups biscuit baking mix
**1 (14-ounce) can Eagle® Brand
  Sweetened Condensed Milk
  (NOT evaporated milk)**
1 egg, beaten
1 teaspoon vanilla extract
**1 to 1½ cups coarsely chopped
  walnuts**
  Confectioners' sugar

Preheat oven to 350°. In large
saucepan, over low heat, melt *1 cup*
chips with margarine; remove from
heat. Add biscuit mix, sweetened
condensed milk, egg and vanilla.
Stir in nuts and remaining *1 cup*
chips. Turn into well-greased 13×9-
inch baking pan. Bake 20 to 25
minutes or until brownies begin to
pull away from sides of pan. Cool.
Sprinkle with confectioners' sugar.
Cut into bars. Store tightly covered
at room temperature.

CHOCOLATE MINT CHEESECAKE BARS

Makes 24 to 36 bars

1¼ cups unsifted flour
1 cup confectioners' sugar
½ cup unsweetened cocoa
¼ teaspoon baking soda
1 cup *cold* margarine or butter
**1 (8-ounce) package cream
  cheese, softened**
**1 (14-ounce) can Eagle® Brand
  Sweetened Condensed Milk
  (NOT evaporated milk)**
2 eggs
1½ teaspoons peppermint extract
  **Green or red food coloring,
  optional**
  Chocolate Glaze

Preheat oven to 350°. In large bowl,
combine flour, sugar, cocoa and
baking soda; cut in margarine until
crumbly (mixture will be dry). Press
firmly on bottom of 13×9-inch
baking pan. Bake 15 minutes.
Meanwhile, in large mixer bowl,
beat cheese until fluffy. Gradually
beat in sweetened condensed milk
until smooth. Add eggs, extract and
food coloring if desired; mix well.
Pour over baked crust. Bake 20
minutes longer or until lightly
browned around edges. Cool.
Drizzle with Chocolate Glaze. Chill.
Cut into bars. Store covered in
refrigerator.

Chocolate Glaze

In small saucepan, over low heat,
melt 2 (1-ounce) squares semi-sweet
chocolate with 2 tablespoons
margarine or butter; stir until
smooth. Remove from heat; stir in
½ teaspoon vanilla extract.
Immediately drizzle over bars.
(Makes about ¼ cup)

STRAWBERRY TUNNEL CREAM CAKE

Makes one 10-inch cake

- **1 (10- or 12-ounce) prepared angel food cake ring**
- **2 (3-ounce) packages cream cheese, softened**
- **1 (14-ounce) can Eagle® Brand Sweetened Condensed Milk (NOT evaporated milk)**
- **⅓ cup ReaLemon® Lemon Juice from Concentrate**
- **1 teaspoon almond extract Red food coloring, optional**
- **1 cup chopped fresh strawberries *or* 1 (16-ounce) package frozen strawberries, thawed and well drained**
- **1 (12-ounce) container frozen non-dairy whipped topping, thawed (5¼ cups) Additional fresh strawberries, optional**

Invert cake onto serving plate. Cut 1-inch slice crosswise from top of cake; set aside. With sharp knife, cut around cake 1 inch from center hole and 1 inch from outer edge, leaving cake walls 1 inch thick. Remove cake from center, leaving 1-inch-thick base on bottom of cake. Tear cake removed from center into bite-size pieces; reserve. In large mixer bowl, beat cheese until fluffy. Gradually beat in sweetened condensed milk until smooth. Stir in ReaLemon® brand, extract and food coloring if desired. Stir in reserved torn cake pieces and chopped strawberries. Fold in *1 cup* whipped topping. Fill cake cavity with strawberry mixture; replace top slice of cake. Frost with remaining whipped topping. Chill 3 hours or freeze 4 hours. Garnish with strawberries if desired. Return leftovers to refrigerator or freezer.

Strawberry Tunnel Cream Cake

Fruited Shortbread Cookies

FRUITED SHORTBREAD COOKIES

Makes about 3 dozen cookies

2½ cups unsifted flour
1 teaspoon baking soda
1 teaspoon cream of tartar
1 cup margarine or butter, softened
1½ cups confectioners' sugar
1 egg
1 (9-ounce) package None Such® Condensed Mincemeat, crumbled
1 teaspoon vanilla extract
Lemon Frosting, optional

Preheat oven to 375°. Combine flour, baking soda and cream of tartar; set aside. In large mixer bowl, beat margarine and sugar until fluffy. Add egg; beat well. Stir in mincemeat and vanilla. Add flour mixture; mix well (dough will be stiff). Roll into 1¼-inch balls. Place on ungreased baking sheets; flatten slightly. Bake 10 to 12 minutes or until lightly browned. Cool. Frost with Lemon Frosting if desired. Garnish as desired.

Lemon Frosting

In small mixer bowl, beat 2 cups confectioners' sugar, 2 tablespoons margarine or butter, softened, 2 tablespoons water and ½ teaspoon grated lemon rind until well blended. (Makes about ⅔ cup)

FUDGE RIBBON CAKE

Makes one 10-inch cake

- 1 (18¼- or 18½-ounce) package chocolate cake mix
- 1 (8-ounce) package cream cheese, softened
- 2 tablespoons margarine or butter, softened
- 1 tablespoon cornstarch
- 1 (14-ounce) can Eagle® Brand Sweetened Condensed Milk (NOT evaporated milk)
- 1 egg
- 1 teaspoon vanilla extract Confectioners' sugar *or* Fudge Glaze

Preheat oven to 350°. Prepare cake mix as package directs. Pour batter into *well-greased* and floured 10-inch fluted tube pan. In small mixer bowl, beat cheese, margarine and cornstarch until fluffy. Gradually beat in sweetened condensed milk then egg and vanilla until smooth. Pour evenly over cake batter. Bake 50 to 55 minutes or until wooden pick inserted near center comes out clean. Cool 15 minutes; remove from pan. Cool. Sprinkle with confectioners' sugar or drizzle with Fudge Glaze.

Fudge Glaze

In small saucepan, over low heat, melt 1 (1-ounce) square unsweetened or semi-sweet chocolate and 1 tablespoon margarine or butter with 2 tablespoons water. Remove from heat. Stir in ¾ cup confectioners' sugar and ½ teaspoon vanilla extract. Stir until smooth and well blended. (Makes about ⅓ cup)

MARBLED CHEESECAKE BARS

Makes 24 to 36 bars

- 2 cups finely crushed creme-filled chocolate sandwich cookies (about 24 cookies)
- 3 tablespoons margarine or butter, melted
- 3 (8-ounce) packages cream cheese, softened
- 1 (14-ounce) can Eagle® Brand Sweetened Condensed Milk (NOT evaporated milk)
- 3 eggs
- 2 teaspoons vanilla extract
- 2 (1-ounce) squares unsweetened chocolate, melted

Preheat oven to 300°. Combine crumbs and margarine; press firmly on bottom of 13×9-inch baking pan. In large mixer bowl, beat cheese until fluffy. Gradually beat in sweetened condensed milk until smooth. Add eggs and vanilla; mix well. Pour half the batter evenly over prepared crust. Stir melted chocolate into remaining batter; spoon over vanilla batter. With table knife or metal spatula, gently swirl through batters to marble. Bake 45 to 50 minutes or until set. Cool. Chill. Cut into bars. Store covered in refrigerator.

Marbled Cheesecake Bars

Cheesecake Topped Brownies

CHEESECAKE TOPPED BROWNIES

Makes 36 to 40 brownies

- 1 (21.5- or 23.6-ounce) package fudge brownie mix
- 1 (8-ounce) package cream cheese, softened
- 2 tablespoons margarine or butter, softened
- 1 tablespoon cornstarch
- 1 (14-ounce) can Eagle® Brand Sweetened Condensed Milk (NOT evaporated milk)
- 1 egg
- 2 teaspoons vanilla extract
  Ready-to-spread chocolate frosting, optional

Preheat oven to 350°. Prepare brownie mix as package directs. Spread into well-greased 13×9-inch baking pan. In small mixer bowl, beat cheese, margarine and cornstarch until fluffy. Gradually beat in sweetened condensed milk then egg and vanilla until smooth. Pour evenly over brownie batter. Bake 45 minutes or until top is lightly browned. Cool. Spread with frosting if desired. Cut into bars. Store covered in refrigerator.

SOUTHERN JAM CAKE

Makes one 9-inch 3-layer cake

- 1 cup margarine or butter, softened
- 1 cup sugar
- 5 eggs
- 1 (16-ounce) jar Bama® Seedless Blackberry Jam
- 1 cup Bama® Strawberry Preserves
- 3 cups unsifted flour
- 1 tablespoon baking soda
- 2 teaspoons ground allspice
- 2 teaspoons ground cinnamon
- 1/2 teaspoon ground cloves
- 1 cup Borden® or Meadow Gold® Buttermilk
  Maple Frosting
  Chopped nuts, optional

Preheat oven to 350°. In large mixer bowl, beat margarine and sugar until fluffy. Add eggs, 1 at a time, beating well after each addition. Stir in jam and preserves. Combine dry ingredients; add alternately with buttermilk to jam mixture. Beat well. Turn into 3 well-greased wax paper-lined 9-inch round layer cake pans. Bake 40 minutes or until wooden pick inserted near centers comes out clean. Cool 5 minutes; remove from pans. Cool completely. Fill and frost with Maple Frosting; garnish with nuts if desired.

Maple Frosting

In mixer bowl, beat 1 (8-ounce) package cream cheese, softened, until fluffy. Add 1 1/2 pounds sifted confectioners' sugar (about 6 cups), 2 teaspoons maple flavoring and 1 tablespoon Borden® or Meadow Gold® Milk; mix well. Add additional milk, 1 teaspoon at a time, for desired consistency. (Makes about 2 1/2 cups)

Easy Piña Colada Cake

EASY PIÑA COLADA CAKE

Makes one 10-inch cake

1 (18¼- to 18½-ounce) package yellow cake mix*
1 (4-serving size) package *instant* vanilla flavor pudding mix
1 (15-ounce) can Coco Lopez® Cream of Coconut
½ cup plus 2 tablespoons rum
⅓ cup vegetable oil
4 eggs
1 (8-ounce) can crushed pineapple, *well drained*
Garnishes: Whipped cream, pineapple chunks, maraschino cherries, toasted coconut

Preheat oven to 350°. In large mixer bowl, combine cake mix, pudding mix, ½ *cup* cream of coconut, ½ *cup* rum, oil and eggs. Beat on medium speed 2 minutes. Stir in pineapple. Pour into *well-greased* and floured 10-inch fluted tube or tube pan. Bake 50 to 55 minutes. Cool 10 minutes; remove from pan. With a table knife or skewer, poke holes about 1 inch apart in cake almost to bottom. Combine remaining cream of coconut and remaining 2 *tablespoons* rum; slowly spoon over cake. Chill thoroughly. Garnish as desired. Store in refrigerator.

**If cake mix with "pudding in" is used, omit pudding mix.*

Chocolate Chip Cheesecake

MINT CHOCOLATE CHIP CHEESECAKE: Omit vanilla. Add ½ to 1 teaspoon peppermint extract and green food coloring if desired. Proceed as directed.

TIP: For best distribution of chips throughout cheesecake, do not oversoften or overbeat cream cheese.

CHOCOLATE CHIP CHEESECAKE

Makes one 9-inch cheesecake

- 1½ cups finely crushed creme-filled chocolate sandwich cookies (about 18 cookies)
- 2 to 3 tablespoons margarine or butter, melted
- 3 (8-ounce) packages cream cheese, softened
- 1 (14-ounce) can Eagle® Brand Sweetened Condensed Milk (NOT evaporated milk)
- 3 eggs
- 2 teaspoons vanilla extract
- 1 cup mini chocolate chips
- 1 teaspoon flour

Preheat oven to 300°. Combine crumbs and margarine; press firmly on bottom of 9-inch springform pan *or* 13×9-inch baking pan. In large mixer bowl, beat cheese until fluffy. Gradually beat in sweetened condensed milk until smooth. Add eggs and vanilla; mix well. In small bowl, toss ½ *cup* chips with flour to coat; stir into cheese mixture. Pour into prepared pan. Sprinkle remaining ½ *cup* chips evenly over top. Bake 1 hour or until center springs back when lightly touched. Turn oven off and allow cheesecake to cool in oven. Chill. Just before serving, remove side of springform pan. Garnish as desired. Refrigerate leftovers.

FUDGE-TOPPED BROWNIES

Makes 36 to 40 brownies

- 1 cup margarine or butter, melted
- 2 cups sugar
- 1 cup unsifted flour
- ⅔ cup unsweetened cocoa
- ½ teaspoon baking powder
- 2 eggs
- ½ cup Borden® or Meadow Gold® Milk
- 3 teaspoons vanilla extract
- 1 cup chopped nuts, optional
- 2 cups (12 ounces) semi-sweet chocolate chips
- 1 (14-ounce) can Eagle® Brand Sweetened Condensed Milk (NOT evaporated milk)
- Dash salt

Preheat oven to 350°. In large mixer bowl, combine margarine, sugar, flour, cocoa, baking powder, eggs, milk and 1½ *teaspoons* vanilla; beat well. Stir in nuts if desired. Spread in greased 13×9-inch baking pan. Bake 40 minutes or until brownies begin to pull away from sides of pan. Just before brownies are done, in heavy medium saucepan, over low heat, melt chips with sweetened condensed milk, remaining 1½ *teaspoons* vanilla and salt. Remove from heat. Immediately spread over hot brownies. Cool. Chill. Cut into bars. Store covered at room temperature.

PECAN PIE BARS

Makes 24 to 36 bars

2 cups unsifted flour
½ cup confectioners' sugar
1 cup *cold* margarine or butter
1 (14-ounce) can Eagle® Brand
Sweetened Condensed Milk
(NOT evaporated milk)
1 egg
1 teaspoon vanilla extract
1 (6-ounce) package almond
brickle chips*
1 cup chopped pecans

Preheat oven to 350° (325° for glass dish). In medium bowl, combine flour and sugar; cut in margarine until crumbly. Press firmly on bottom of 13×9-inch baking pan. Bake 15 minutes. Meanwhile, in medium bowl, beat sweetened condensed milk, egg and vanilla. Stir in chips and pecans. Spread evenly over baked crust. Bake 25 minutes or until golden brown. Cool. Cut into bars. Store covered in refrigerator.

If desired, omit almond brickle chips; increase pecans to 2 cups.

Pecan Pie Bars

Lemon Blossom Cookies

LEMON BLOSSOM COOKIES

Makes about 6 dozen cookies

2 cups margarine or butter,
softened
1½ cups confectioners' sugar
¼ cup ReaLemon® Lemon Juice
from Concentrate
4 cups unsifted flour
Finely chopped nuts, optional
Assorted Bama® Fruit Jams and
Preserves or pecan halves

Preheat oven to 350°. In large mixer bowl, beat margarine and sugar until fluffy. Add ReaLemon® brand; beat well. Gradually add flour; mix well. Cover; chill 2 hours. Shape into 1-inch balls; roll in nuts if desired. Place 1 inch apart on greased baking sheets. Press thumb in center of each ball; fill with jam or pecan. Bake 14 to 16 minutes or until lightly browned. Cool. Store covered at room temperature.

Sour Cream Brownie Cake

Fudgy Frosting

In small mixer bowl, beat 2 cups confectioners' sugar, ½ cup Borden® or Meadow Gold® Sour Cream, 1 tablespoon butter or margarine, softened, 2 (1-ounce) squares unsweetened chocolate, melted, and 1 teaspoon vanilla until smooth. (Makes about 1½ cups)

SOUR CREAM BROWNIE CAKE

Makes one 15×10-inch sheet cake

- 1 cup butter or margarine
- 2 (1-ounce) squares unsweetened chocolate
- 1 cup water
- 2 cups firmly packed brown sugar
- 2 cups unsifted flour
- 1 teaspoon baking soda
- ½ teaspoon salt
- 1 (8-ounce) container Borden® or Meadow Gold® Sour Cream
- 2 eggs
- 1 tablespoon vanilla extract
- 1 cup chopped nuts, optional
  Fudgy Frosting

Preheat oven to 350°. Melt butter and chocolate with water; cool. Combine dry ingredients; set aside. In large mixer bowl, beat sour cream, eggs, vanilla and chocolate mixture. Add flour mixture; beat until smooth. Add nuts if desired. Pour into greased and floured 15×10-inch baking pan. Bake 25 minutes or until wooden pick inserted in center comes out clean. Cool. Frost with Fudgy Frosting. Refrigerate. Store covered in refrigerator.

MAHOGANY POUND CAKE

Makes one 10-inch cake

- 2½ cups unsifted flour
- ½ cup unsweetened cocoa
- ¼ teaspoon baking soda
- 2 cups granulated sugar
- 1 cup firmly packed light brown sugar
- 1½ cups butter or margarine, softened
- 6 eggs, *separated*
- 1 teaspoon vanilla extract
- 1 (8-ounce) container Borden® or Meadow Gold® Sour Cream

Preheat oven to 325°. Combine flour, cocoa and baking soda; set aside. In large mixer bowl, beat sugars and butter until fluffy. Add egg *yolks*, 1 at a time, beating well after each addition; add vanilla. Beat in sour cream alternately with dry ingredients (batter is very thick). In medium bowl, beat egg *whites* until stiff but not dry; fold half into batter. Fold in remaining egg whites until blended. Pour into *well-greased* and floured 10-inch tube or fluted tube pan. Bake 1½ hours or until wooden pick inserted near center comes out clean. Cool 10 minutes; remove from pan. Sprinkle with confectioners' sugar if desired.

FUDGE TRUFFLE CHEESECAKE

Makes one 9-inch cheesecake

Chocolate Crumb Crust
3 (8-ounce) packages cream cheese, softened
1 (14-ounce) can Eagle® Brand Sweetened Condensed Milk (NOT evaporated milk)
2 cups (12 ounces) semi-sweet chocolate chips *or* 8 (1-ounce) squares semi-sweet chocolate, melted
4 eggs
¼ cup coffee-flavored liqueur, optional
2 teaspoons vanilla extract

Preheat oven to 300°. Prepare Chocolate Crumb Crust. In large mixer bowl, beat cheese until fluffy. Gradually beat in sweetened condensed milk until smooth. Add remaining ingredients; mix well. Pour into prepared pan. Bake 1 hour and 5 minutes or until center is set. Cool. Chill. Just before serving, remove side of springform pan. Garnish as desired. Refrigerate leftovers.

Chocolate Crumb Crust

In medium bowl, combine 1½ cups vanilla wafer crumbs (about 45 wafers), ½ cup confectioners' sugar, ⅓ cup unsweetened cocoa and ⅓ cup margarine or butter, melted. Press firmly on bottom of 9-inch springform pan.

DOUBLE DELICIOUS COOKIE BARS

Makes 24 to 36 bars

½ cup margarine or butter
1½ cups graham cracker crumbs
1 (14-ounce) can Eagle® Brand Sweetened Condensed Milk (NOT evaporated milk)
2 cups (12 ounces) semi-sweet chocolate chips
1 cup peanut butter chips
Quick Chocolate Glaze, optional

Preheat oven to 350° (325° for glass dish). In 13×9-inch baking pan, melt margarine in oven. Sprinkle crumbs evenly over margarine; pour sweetened condensed milk evenly over crumbs. Top with chips; press down firmly. Bake 25 to 30 minutes or until lightly browned. Cool. Drizzle with Quick Chocolate Glaze if desired. Cut into bars. Store loosely covered at room temperature.

Quick Chocolate Glaze

In small saucepan, melt 1 cup (6 ounces) semi-sweet chocolate chips with 1½ teaspoons shortening. Immediately drizzle over bars. (Makes about ½ cup)

Double Delicious Cookie Bars

COOL & CREAMY CREATIONS

FRESH FRUIT ICE CREAM

Makes about 1½ quarts

- 3 cups (1½ pints) Borden® or Meadow Gold® Half-and-Half
- 1 (14-ounce) can Eagle® Brand Sweetened Condensed Milk (NOT evaporated milk)
- 1 cup puréed or mashed fresh fruit (peaches, strawberries, bananas, raspberries, etc.)
- 1 tablespoon vanilla extract
  Food coloring, optional

In ice cream freezer container, combine all ingredients; mix well. Freeze according to manufacturer's instructions. Freeze leftovers.

VANILLA ICE CREAM: Omit fruit and food coloring. Increase half-and-half to 4 cups. Proceed as above.

REFRIGERATOR-FREEZER METHOD: Omit half-and-half. In large bowl, combine sweetened condensed milk and vanilla; stir in 1 cup puréed or mashed fruit and food coloring if desired. Fold in 2 cups (1 pint) Borden® or Meadow Gold® Whipping Cream, whipped (*do not use non-dairy whipped topping*). Pour into 9×5-inch loaf pan or other 2-quart container; cover. Freeze 6 hours or until firm. Freeze leftovers.

HOT FUDGE SAUCE

Makes about 2 cups

- 1 cup (6 ounces) semi-sweet chocolate chips *or*
  4 (1-ounce) squares semi-sweet chocolate
- 2 tablespoons margarine or butter
- 1 (14-ounce) can Eagle® Brand Sweetened Condensed Milk (NOT evaporated milk)
- 2 tablespoons water
- 1 teaspoon vanilla extract

In small heavy saucepan, over medium heat, melt chips and margarine with sweetened condensed milk and water. Cook and stir constantly until thickened, about 5 minutes. Add vanilla. Serve warm over ice cream or as a fruit dipping sauce. Refrigerate leftovers.

TO REHEAT: In small heavy saucepan, combine desired amount of sauce with small amount of water. Over low heat, stir constantly until heated through.

MICROWAVE: In 1-quart glass measure with handle, combine ingredients. Cook on 100% power (high) 3 to 3½ minutes, stirring after each minute. Proceed as above.

Peach and Strawberry Fresh Fruit Ice Creams

Left to right: Banana Split Squares and Peach Melba Parfaits

PEACH MELBA PARFAITS

Makes 6 to 8 parfaits

- ¾ cup quick-cooking oats
- ⅓ cup firmly packed light brown sugar
- ⅓ cup silvered almonds, toasted
- ⅓ cup unsifted flour
- ¼ cup margarine or butter, melted
- ½ teaspoon ground cinnamon
- 1 (10-ounce) package frozen red raspberries in light syrup, thawed
- ¼ cup Bama® Red Raspberry Preserves or Red Currant Jelly
- 1 tablespoon cornstarch
- 2 tablespoons amaretto liqueur
- ½ (½-gallon) carton Borden® or Meadow Gold® Peach Premium Frozen Yogurt, slightly softened

Preheat oven to 350°. Combine oats, sugar, nuts, flour, margarine and cinnamon; mix well. Spread in 9-inch baking pan; bake 10 to 15 minutes or until golden. Stir; cool. In blender or food processor container, purée raspberries. In small saucepan, combine puréed raspberries, preserves and cornstarch. Over medium heat, cook and stir until slightly thickened and glossy. Stir in amaretto; cool. In parfait or dessert glasses, layer half *each* of the raspberry sauce, frozen yogurt then oat mixture; repeat layers. Freeze. Remove from freezer 5 to 10 minutes before serving. Garnish as desired. Freeze leftovers.

BANANA SPLIT SQUARES

Makes 12 to 16 servings

1 (21.5- or 23.6-ounce) package fudge brownie mix
2 bananas, thinly sliced, dipped in ReaLemon® Lemon Juice from Concentrate and drained
½ cup chopped nuts, optional
2 quarts and 1 pint Borden® or Meadow Gold® Ice Cream, any 3 flavors, softened
Garnishes: Chocolate ice cream topping, whipped cream, banana slices, nuts, cherries

Preheat oven to 350°. Prepare brownie mix as package directs; spread in 13×9-inch baking pan. Bake 20 to 25 minutes; cool. On top of baked brownie, layer bananas, nuts if desired, *1 quart* ice cream, *1 pint* ice cream and *1 quart* ice cream. Cover; freeze 6 hours or until firm. Remove from freezer 10 minutes before serving. Cut into squares; garnish as desired. Freeze leftovers.

FROZEN PASSION

Makes 2 to 3 quarts

2 (14-ounce) cans Eagle® Brand Sweetened Condensed Milk (NOT evaporated milk)
1 (2-liter) bottle *or* 5 (12-ounce) cans carbonated beverage, any flavor

In ice cream freezer container, combine ingredients; mix well. Freeze according to manufacturer's instructions. Freeze leftovers.

Creamy Banana Pudding

CREAMY BANANA PUDDING

Makes 8 to 10 servings

1 (14-ounce) can Eagle® Brand Sweetened Condensed Milk (NOT evaporated milk)
1½ cups cold water
1 (4-serving size) package *instant* vanilla flavor pudding mix
2 cups (1 pint) Borden® or Meadow Gold® Whipping Cream, whipped
36 vanilla wafers
3 medium bananas, sliced and dipped in ReaLemon® Lemon Juice from Concentrate

In large bowl, combine sweetened condensed milk and water. Add pudding mix; beat well. Chill 5 minutes. Fold in whipped cream. Spoon *1 cup* pudding mixture into 2½-quart glass serving bowl. Top with one-third *each* of the wafers, bananas and pudding. Repeat layering twice, ending with pudding. Cover; chill. Garnish as desired. Refrigerate leftovers.

TIP: Mixture can be layered in individual serving dishes.

Creamy Lemon and Lime Sherbets

CREAMY LEMON SHERBET

Makes about 3 cups

1 cup sugar
2 cups (1 pint) Borden® or
   Meadow Gold® Whipping
   Cream, *unwhipped*
½ cup ReaLemon® Lemon Juice
   from Concentrate
   Yellow food coloring, optional

In medium bowl, combine sugar
and cream, stirring until dissolved.
Stir in ReaLemon® brand and food
coloring if desired. Pour into 8-inch
square pan or directly into sherbet
dishes. Freeze 3 hours or until firm.
Remove from freezer 5 minutes
before serving. Freeze leftovers.

LIME SHERBET: Substitute ReaLime®
Lime Juice from Concentrate for
ReaLemon® brand and green food
coloring for yellow.

BROWNIE MINT SUNDAE SQUARES

Makes 10 to 12 servings

1 (21.5- or 23.6-ounce) package
   fudge brownie mix
¾ cup coarsely chopped walnuts
1 (14-ounce) can Eagle® Brand
   Sweetened Condensed Milk
   (NOT evaporated milk)
2 teaspoons peppermint extract
   Green food coloring, optional
2 cups (1 pint) Borden® or
   Meadow Gold® Whipping
   Cream, whipped
½ cup mini chocolate chips

Prepare brownie mix as package
directs; stir in walnuts. Turn into
aluminum foil-lined and greased
13×9-inch baking pan. Bake as
directed. Cool thoroughly. In large
bowl, combine sweetened
condensed milk, extract and food
coloring if desired. Fold in whipped
cream and chips. Pour over brownie
layer. Cover; freeze 6 hours or until
firm. To serve, lift from pan with foil;
cut into squares. Serve with Hot
Fudge Sauce (see page 84) or
chocolate ice cream topping if
desired. Garnish as desired. Freeze
leftovers.

Brownie Mint Sundae Squares and
Hot Fudge Sauce (page 84)

Fudgy Chocolate Ice Cream

FUDGY CHOCOLATE ICE CREAM

Makes about 1½ quarts

5 (1-ounce) squares unsweetened chocolate, melted
1 (14-ounce) can Eagle® Brand Sweetened Condensed Milk (NOT evaporated milk)
2 teaspoons vanilla extract
2 cups (1 pint) Borden® or Meadow Gold® Half-and-Half
2 cups (1 pint) Borden® or Meadow Gold® Whipping Cream, *unwhipped*
½ cup chopped nuts, optional

In large mixer bowl, beat chocolate, sweetened condensed milk and vanilla until well blended. Stir in half-and-half, whipping cream and nuts if desired. Pour into ice cream freezer container. Freeze according to manufacturer's instructions. Freeze leftovers.

REFRIGERATOR-FREEZER METHOD: Omit half-and-half. Reduce chocolate to 3 (1-ounce) squares. Whip whipping cream. In large mixer bowl, beat chocolate, sweetened condensed milk and vanilla until well blended; fold in whipped cream and nuts if desired. Pour into 9×5-inch loaf pan or other 2-quart container; cover. Freeze 6 hours or until firm. Freeze leftovers.

LUSCIOUS LEMON CREAM

Makes about 3 cups

2 eggs
1 cup sugar
⅓ cup ReaLemon® Lemon Juice from Concentrate
1 tablespoon cornstarch
½ cup water
1 teaspoon vanilla extract
1 cup (½ pint) Borden® or Meadow Gold® Whipping Cream, whipped

In small bowl, beat eggs, ½ cup sugar and ReaLemon® brand until frothy; set aside. In medium saucepan, combine remaining ½ cup sugar and cornstarch. Gradually add water; mix well. Over medium heat, cook and stir until thickened and clear; remove from heat. Gradually beat in egg mixture. Over low heat, cook and stir until slightly thickened. Remove from heat; add vanilla. Cool. Fold whipped cream into sauce. Cover; chill. Serve with fresh fruit. Refrigerate leftovers.

Luscious Lemon Cream

Index

Tips & Techniques

How to Caramelize Eagle® Brand Sweetened Condensed Milk

Oven Method: Preheat oven to 425°. Pour sweetened condensed milk into 8- or 9-inch pie plate. Cover with aluminum foil; place in shallow pan. Fill pan with hot water. Bake 1 to 1 1/2 hours or until thick and light caramel-colored. Remove foil; cool. Chill thoroughly.

Microwave Method: Pour sweetened condensed milk into 2-quart glass measure with handle. Cook on 50% power (medium) 4 minutes, stirring after 2 minutes. Reduce to 30% power (medium-low); cook 12 to 18 minutes or until thick and light caramel-colored, stirring briskly every 2 minutes until smooth. Cool. Chill thoroughly.

*CAUTION: NEVER HEAT UNOPENED CAN

To serve as a pudding, top with chopped nuts, whipped cream or shaved chocolate. Can also be used as a topping with fruit, ice cream, pound cake or baked apples or to fill cream puffs or cake layers.

Whipping Cream

Chill bowl and beaters thoroughly.

Beat chilled whipping cream on high speed. Beat only until stiff. (Overbeating or beating on low speed can cause cream to separate into fat and liquid).

Whipping cream doubles in volume when beaten.

To sweeten whipped cream, gradually beat in 1 to 2 tablespoons granulated or confectioners' sugar and 1/2 to 1 teaspoon vanilla extract for each cup unwhipped whipping cream.

Helpful Hints

If your recipe calls for 1 cup broth or stock, dissolve 1 teaspoon Wyler's® or Steero® Instant Bouillon *or* 1 Bouillon Cube in 1 cup boiling water.

In any recipe calling for the juice of one lemon, use 3 to 4 tablespoons ReaLemon® Lemon Juice from Concentrate. Substitute 2 to 3 tablespoons ReaLime® brand for the juice of 1 lime.

To cut down on sodium, sprinkle ReaLemon® Lemon Juice from Concentrate instead of salt on fish, chicken or vegetables to enhance the flavor.

To keep apple wedges, banana slices and other fruit from darkening, dip in ReaLemon® brand.

To toast coconut or nuts, spread evenly in shallow pan. Toast in preheated 350° oven 7 to 15 minutes or until golden, stirring frequently.

NOTES

NOTES

METRIC CONVERSION CHART

VOLUME MEASUREMENT (dry)

⅛ teaspoon = .5 mL
¼ teaspoon = 1 mL
½ teaspoon = 2 mL
¾ teaspoon = 4 mL
1 teaspoon = 5 mL
1 tablespoon = 15 mL
2 tablespoons = 25 mL
¼ cup = 50 mL
⅓ cup = 75 mL
⅔ cup = 150 mL
¾ cup = 175 mL
1 cup = 250 mL
2 cups = 1 pint = 500 mL
3 cups = 750 mL
4 cups = 1 quart = 1 L

DIMENSION

1/16 inch = 2 mm
⅛ inch = 3 mm
¼ inch = 6 mm
½ inch = 1.5 cm
¾ inch = 2 cm
1 inch = 2.5 cm

OVEN TEMPERATURES

250°F = 120°C
275°F = 140°C
300°F = 150°C
325°F = 160°C
350°F = 180°C
375°F = 190°C
400°F = 200°C
425°F = 220°C
450°F = 230°C

VOLUME MEASUREMENT (fluid)

1 fluid ounce (2 tablespoons) = 30 mL
4 fluid ounces (½ cup) = 125 mL
8 fluid ounces (1 cup) = 250 mL
12 fluid ounces (1½ cups) = 375 mL
16 fluid ounces (2 cups) = 500 mL

BAKING PAN SIZES

Utensil	Inches/ Quarts	Metric Volume	Centimeters
Baking or	8 × 8 × 2	2 L	20 × 20 × 5
Cake pan	9 × 9 × 2	2.5 L	22 × 22 × 5
(square or	12 × 8 × 2	3 L	30 × 20 × 5
rectangular)	13 × 9 × 2	3.5 L	33 × 23 × 5
Loaf Pan	8 × 4 × 3	1.5 L	20 × 10 × 7
	9 × 5 × 3	2 L	23 × 13 × 7
Round Layer	8 × 1½	1.2 L	20 × 4
Cake Pan	9 × 1½	1.5 L	23 × 4
Pie Plate	8 × 1¼	750 mL	20 × 3
	9 × 1¼	1 L	23 × 3
Baking Dish	1 quart	1 L	
or	1½ quart	1.5 L	
Casserole	2 quart	2 L	

WEIGHT (MASS)

½ ounce = 15 g
1 ounce = 30 g
3 ounces = 85 g
3.75 ounces = 100 g
4 ounces = 115 g
8 ounces = 225 g
12 ounces = 340 g
16 ounces = 1 pound = 450 g